The 5-Minute BIBLE STUDY for Men

YOU are the reason we do what we do here at Barbour Publishing. We promise that we will always use our God-given talents to produce content with you in mind—and that we will remain biblically faithful, no matter what.

Thank you for being the heart of our business.

ISBN 979-8-89151-270-2

Published by Barbour Publishing, Inc., 1810 Barbour Drive, Uhrichsville, Ohio 44683, www.barbourbooks.com

Our mission is to inspire the world with the life-changing message of the Bible.

Printed in the United States of America.

Tracy M. Sumner

The 5-Minute BIBLE STUDY for Men

Pursuing
a Life
That Matters

Introduction

Do you find it hard to make time for Bible study? You intend to do it, but the hours turn into days; before you know it, another week has passed and you have not picked up God's Word. This book provides an avenue for you to open the Bible regularly and dig into a passage—even if you have only five minutes! Here's how it works:

- Minutes 1–2: ***Read*** carefully the scripture passage for each day's Bible study.
- Minute 3: ***Understand.*** Ponder a couple of prompts designed to help you apply the verses from the Bible to your own life. Consider these throughout your day as well.
- Minute 4: ***Apply.*** Read a devotion based on the day's scriptural focus.
- Minute 5: ***Pray.*** A prayer starter will help you begin a time of conversation with God. Remember to allow time for Him to speak into your life as well.

May *The 5-Minute Bible Study for Men* help you establish the discipline of studying God's Word. Head out to your car or truck five minutes early with this book and your Bible. Your willingness to spend these minutes focused on God's Word and prayer can make a huge difference in your day!

It's All About Faith

Read Hebrews 11:1–12

Key Verse:

And without faith it is impossible to please God, because anyone who comes to him must believe that he exists and that he rewards those who earnestly seek him.

HEBREWS 11:6 NIV

Understand:

- Why is a man's faith so important to the Lord?
- What are some of the benefits of unflinching faith in the Lord?

Apply:

Hebrews 11 is often called the "Hall of Faith" because it recounts the exploits of Old Testament saints whose faith motivated and enabled them to do great things for the Lord and for His people, often in very challenging circumstances. This chapter cites several men and women of faith, including Abel, Enoch, Noah, Abraham, Sarah, Isaac, Jacob, Moses, Rahab, Gideon, Barak, Samson, and Jephthah.

These were not perfect people (some of them, in fact, were deeply flawed), but they believed in God and earnestly sought Him, making them examples of the instructions in today's key verse to "believe that [God] exists" and to "earnestly seek him."

Hebrews 11:6 begins with the truth that "without faith it is impossible to please God," meaning that faith is foundational to our relationship with the Lord. If we want to please Him, we must trust Him. And if we trust Him, we'll seek Him, knowing that He will reward us for doing so.

If you want to please the Lord in every way, then build your life around a strong faith in Him. You can do that when you seek Him with your whole heart and ask Him to instill in your heart and mind a Hebrews 11 kind of faith.

Pray:

Lord Jesus, please strengthen my faith daily so that I can love You from my heart and please You in every way.

Humble Servants. . . like Jesus

Read Philippians 2:1-11

Key Verses:

Do nothing out of selfish ambition or vain conceit. Rather, in humility value others above yourselves, not looking to your own interests but each of you to the interests of the others.

PHILIPPIANS 2:3–4 NIV

Understand:

- In what ways did Jesus serve others when He was here on earth?
- In what ways can you begin valuing others and serving others above yourself today?

Apply:

Jesus once defined His mission on earth when He said to His followers, "The Son of Man did not come to be served, but to serve, and to give his life as a ransom for many" (Matthew 20:28 NIV). Our Savior came to perform the humblest and most selfless act in all of eternity, namely dying on a cross so that we could be forgiven of our sins and inherit a place in His eternal kingdom.

Jesus' servant Paul encouraged the Philippian Christians—and now us—toward a radical approach to their relationships with one another when he wrote that they should "have the same mindset as Christ Jesus" (Philippians 2:5 NIV).

In that same scripture passage, Paul described a Jesus who took "the form of a slave, taking on the likeness of men" and who then "humbled Himself by becoming obedient to the point of death—even to death on a cross" (Philippians 2:8 HCSB). Our attitude is to be like that of Jesus, whose whole focus was serving. We're to have His attitude of self-denial and self-sacrifice on behalf of others.

Pray:

Lord Jesus, I want to humbly give and serve like You did. Help me to see myself as the servant of others, just like You were. Help me to be on the lookout for opportunities to sacrifice myself for others.

Created Anew for Good Things

Read Ephesians 2:1-10

Key Verse:

For we are God's masterpiece. He has created us anew in Christ Jesus, so we can do the good things he planned for us long ago.

EPHESIANS 2:10 NLT

Understand:

- What impresses you most about classic art masterpieces?
- What good things has God created you anew for in this life?

Apply:

If you've ever taken the time to truly appreciate fine classic artworks—for example, Van Gogh's *The Starry Night,* Rembrandt's *The Storm on the Sea of Galilee,* or Leonardo da Vinci's *Mona Lisa,* then you may have found yourself in awe of the individual artist's skill, imagination, and passion for his work.

These works of art are considered masterpieces not just because of their obvious quality but because of who painted them—people who have come to be known as masters of their craft.

The key verse in this study calls you and every other follower of Jesus a "masterpiece," with our Father in heaven the master artist. He has done for us what only He could do: take men who were completely dead in their sins and miraculously make them alive and able to do good works for Him.

The Bible teaches that we are saved only as a result of God's amazing grace, not as the result of anything good or worthy about us (Ephesians 2:8–9). But God didn't "[create] us anew in Christ Jesus" so we can just wait around to enter God's eternal, heavenly kingdom. As God's masterpieces, we are called to glorify the Lord by doing good things, things He planned for us long before we were even born.

What an amazing privilege! What an amazing calling!

Pray:

Jesus, thank You for making me Your own masterpiece. Show me the good works You have planned for me so that I can bring glory to Your wonderful name.

A Well-Armed Believer

Read Ephesians 6:10–18

Key Verse:

Put on the full armor of God, so that you can take your stand against the devil's schemes.

Ephesians 6:11 NIV

Understand:

- What is the nature of the warfare Christians fight in this world?
- What are your weapons of spiritual warfare, according to Ephesians 6:10–18?

Apply:

At present, the devil has power in this world, and the results are obvious and everywhere. On our own, we are no match for the evil one and are doomed to defeat. This is war, and the enemy is too powerful and too well armed for us to stand any chance of victory.

But the Bible tells us that we've not been left to fight on our own. In Ephesians 6:10–18, Paul listed an array of spiritual weapons we have at our disposal and how they equip us for spiritual warfare:

- The belt of truth so you won't be vulnerable to the enemy's lies

- The breastplate of righteousness to guard your heart from sin and unrighteousness
- The footwear of the gospel of peace so you can stand on the truth of God's Word
- The shield of faith, which protects you from the evil one's attacks
- The helmet of salvation to guard your thoughts
- The sword of the Spirit (the Word of God) as a weapon to defeat the enemy's lies
- Prayer, which enables you to take all your concerns and problems directly to the Lord

There truly is a war going on out there in the world. But God has given you everything you need for victory.

Pray:

Lord, I arm myself again today to fight the battles of the spirit. The fight is real and of great consequence, but You have given me everything I need to win.

Overcoming the Evil One

Read 1 John 2:12-17

Key Verse:

I am writing to you, fathers, because you know him who is from the beginning. I am writing to you, young men, because you have overcome the evil one.

1 John 2:13 NIV

Understand:

- What great promises are found in today's scripture passage?
- In what ways does John affirm and encourage Christians in their faith in this passage?

Apply:

In verses 12–14 of this study's scripture passage, the apostle John listed several amazing benefits of a life of faith in Jesus Christ, twice including the promise that we have "overcome the evil one."

Ephesians 6:12 (NIV) tells us believers that "our struggle is not against flesh and blood, but against the rulers, against the authorities, against the powers of this dark world and against the spiritual forces of evil in the heavenly realms."

This is a good definition of what is called spiritual

warfare—a war John said we can win when we grow in our relationship with Jesus and keep ourselves in God's Word. Our ultimate spiritual enemy, the devil, has already lost the biggest battle with those of us who trust Jesus as our Lord and Savior. Now his goal is to keep us from living a victorious life of faith and obedience.

But when we cling to Jesus and live by God's Word, we can be "more than conquerors" (Romans 8:37 NIV) as we live each and every day in His fulfilled promise of the final and complete defeat of the enemy of our souls.

Pray:

Lord Jesus, may I always cling to You and Your truth, knowing that I have overcome the devil. May I live a victorious life of faith and courage.

The True Vine

Read John 15:1-11

Key Verse:

"I am the vine; you are the branches. If you remain in me and I in you, you will bear much fruit; apart from me you can do nothing."

JOHN 15:5 NIV

Understand:

- Who is the gardener in this parable in John 15:1–11?
- What does it mean to you to remain in Jesus? What are the results of doing so?

Apply:

In the first-century largely agrarian land of Israel, Jesus' twelve disciples may not have understood the science we now call botany, but they had a good grasp of how plants produce fruit. They knew that branches couldn't produce fruit unless they were attached to the main vine.

As the Creator of all things, Jesus understood this biological truth better than anyone, and He used it to teach His followers that He didn't expect them to do any of the great things He had called them to do under their own power. That is why He told them, "If you remain in me and I in you, you will bear much fruit;

apart from me you can do nothing."

This wonderful truth applies to us today as well. If we want to live the lives God wants us to live and do for Him and His kingdom the things He has called us to do, we'll need to remain in close fellowship with Jesus each and every day. Otherwise, we can do nothing of eternal value for Him.

Pray:

Jesus, thank You for being my vine. Remind me often to cling to You and depend on You daily so that I can do the things You've called me to do, for without You, even my best efforts are in vain.

A New Creation

Read 2 Corinthians 5:11-21

Key Verse:

Therefore, if anyone is in Christ, the new creation has come: The old has gone, the new is here!

2 Corinthians 5:17 NIV

Understand:

- In what ways has becoming a new creation transformed you?
- What does it mean to you to be reconciled to God through Jesus Christ?

Apply:

How much thought have you given to who you are in Christ? Not to the ways He has changed you, though those changes are certainly reasons to praise Him, but to how He has completely transformed you into something you weren't before He saved you and gave you His Holy Spirit.

God did something only He could do when you came to faith in Jesus. He took a helpless, lost, sin-filled, spiritually dead creature and gave it a new life, a new identity, a new way of thinking, and a new purpose. You may look like the same person. Your personality may be mostly the same. But the way you think and live and relate to Him and others has been not just changed but *transformed*. That's because Jesus lives inside you in the person of the Holy Spirit, and that changes everything.

That's what the apostle Paul meant when he called us "the new creation."

But it doesn't end there. Over time, day by day, God makes you more and more like Jesus. Your old way of thinking and living is replaced by something much better: the abundant life that Jesus promised you!

Pray:

Dear Jesus, thank You for making me a new creation. You've done what I could never do for myself. Thank You for replacing the sinful, dark side of me with a heart that pursues You and what You want in me.

Faith That Works

Read James 2:14-26

Key Verses:

So you see, faith by itself isn't enough. Unless it produces good deeds, it is dead and useless. Now someone may argue, "Some people have faith; others have good deeds." But I say, "How can you show me your faith if you don't have good deeds? I will show you my faith by my good deeds."

James 2:17–18 NLT

Understand:

- On what basis did God save you and set you on the path to an eternity in heaven?
- How are saving faith and good works related?

Apply:

The Bible is abundantly clear that God saves us and makes us His people on the basis of faith in the Lord Jesus Christ and not because of any of our own good works. Paul stated this truth without equivocation when he wrote, "For it is by grace you have been saved, through faith—and this is not from yourselves, it is the gift of God—not by works, so that no one can boast" (Ephesians 2:8–9 NIV).

A quick reading of James 2:14–26 might seem to contradict God's message of salvation through faith alone. But James was not saying that we are saved through faith *plus* our good works but that our faith should *result* in acts of charity and compassion.

Paul stated this same truth in Ephesians 2, immediately after verses 8–9 (his declaration that believers are saved through faith alone): "For we are God's handiwork, created in Christ Jesus to do good works, which God prepared in advance for us to do" (verse 10 NIV).

We live in a world filled with hurting, needy people. We should live out our faith by tending to those who need to see a faith that works.

Pray:

Lord Jesus, thank You for saving me through my faith in You. May my faith result in good works that glorify You and bless others.

Trust and Obey

Read Leviticus 26:1-13

Key Verses:

"I will walk among you; I will be your God, and you will be my people. I am the LORD your God, who brought you out of the land of Egypt so you would no longer be their slaves. I broke the yoke of slavery from your neck so you can walk with your heads held high."

LEVITICUS 26:12–13 NLT

Understand:

- What did God require of the Israelites in order for Him to walk among them?
- What great things does God remind His people of in this passage?

Apply:

In John 14:15 (NLT), Jesus told His disciples, "If you love me, obey my commandments." Jesus' statement tells us that *obedience* marks a believer who is in a place in his faith life where he can truly enjoy Christ's loving presence.

The same thing was true for the Israelites who had been freed from slavery in Egypt thousands of years before the arrival of the Messiah.

The book of Leviticus contains the laws and statutes and commands that God had given His chosen people as they left Egypt. As it draws to a close, the Lord makes a series of promises regarding rewards and blessings attached to obedience to His commands. All the laws, rules, commandments, and statutes made it possible for the Israelites to be God's people and to enjoy His presence with them.

In today's scripture passage, we see that obedience to God's commands would lead to various blessings. We Christian men can enjoy similar blessings today—including God's presence with us—as long as we don't just *hear* God's Word but also *do* it (see James 1:22).

Pray:

Lord God, thank You that You have promised that when I walk in obedience, You will be with me as I make my way through this journey called life.

Content with God's Provision

Read Hebrews 13:1-8

Key Verse:

Don't love money; be satisfied with what you have. For God has said, "I will never fail you. I will never abandon you."
HEBREWS 13:5 NLT

Understand:

- What is your attitude toward money and the hard work it takes to earn it?
- How can you develop an attitude of contentment with what you have?

Apply:

The Bible has much to say about earthly riches (money and other assets), and it is largely very positive. The ability to earn money is a blessing from God, and there's absolutely nothing wrong with men working hard to provide for themselves and their families.

But Hebrews 13:5 warns its readers against loving money and then finishes with these encouraging words: "For God has said, 'I will never fail you. I will never abandon you.'" The word *For* in this wonderfully truthful statement suggests something about greed and discontentment, and it's this: When we followers of Christ lose sight of God's promises to care for us, it's easier to fall into the trap of discontentment. And when discontentment takes hold, we're more vulnerable to greed. That, according to 1 Timothy 6:10, leads to some very bad things in a man's life.

It is a good and godly thing to work hard and make money to care for your needs and your family's needs. God blesses that and even commands it. Nowhere in His written Word is hard work for financial gain condemned or discouraged. But let's always remember that we believers are cared for and therefore shouldn't be preoccupied with money.

So trust in God to meet all your needs. He will never fail you!

Pray:

Lord Jesus, may I always feel content with what I have and rest in knowing that You have promised never to fail me or abandon me.

Asking and Receiving

Read John 16:20-28

Key Verses:

"Very truly I tell you, my Father will give you whatever you ask in my name. Until now you have not asked for anything in my name. Ask and you will receive, and your joy will be complete."

JOHN 16:23–24 NIV

Understand:

- What have you been asking God to do for you lately?
- How can you know if your prayer requests are in accordance with God's will?

Apply:

In today's key verses, Jesus encouraged His followers to make their prayer requests to God "in my name" and to expect that they would receive what they asked for.

Jesus had taught the disciples about prayer, but in this study's key verses, He took His teaching to a new level when He instructed them to bring their requests to the Father in His, Jesus', name. So praying in Jesus' name is obviously a good thing. But it's important to pay attention to the purpose behind this promise: "So that the Son can bring glory to the Father" (John 14:13 NLT).

Jesus never promised to give us everything we want when we pray in His name. Praying for a brand-new, top-of-the-line automobile *probably* won't yield the results we're hoping for, as this likely isn't God's will. Nor is God obligated to bless you with a fat bank account or a huge house, simply because you ask in Jesus' name.

Instead, Jesus promised to do what we ask, but only when it glorifies God. So before you bring your requests to God in Jesus' name, search your heart and ask yourself, *Does this request glorify God?* If the answer is yes, then ask. . .in Jesus' name!

Pray:

Dear Jesus, thank You for giving me access to the Father so that I can make my requests known to Him. May all my requests be for those things that glorify God.

A Heart of Gratitude

Read 1 Thessalonians 5:12-22

Key Verse:

Be thankful in all circumstances, for this is God's will for you who belong to Christ Jesus.

1 Thessalonians 5:18 NLT

Understand:

- How do you typically respond during difficult times?
- How can you best maintain a thankful heart?

Apply:

It's easy to speak words of gratitude from the heart when it feels like life is treating us well—when our work life and financial situation seem in order, when we and those we love are in good health, when we are happy and content in our human relationships, when. . .well, you can fill in the blank for yourself.

But what about those times when life fills us with crushing inner turmoil, when we just can't see how anything good can come out of our present circumstances?

Jesus made many wonderful promises during His earthly ministry, one of which we may sometimes wish He hadn't: "In this world you will have trouble" (John

16:33 NIV). Life in Christ here on earth isn't always easy. We will face difficulties and suffering, but today's key verse tells how we can not only survive but thrive when life isn't easy.

Being "thankful in all circumstances" doesn't mean that we give God thanks *for* all things but rather *in* all things. It means that even when we are suffering, stressed out, and in serious need, we can go to God and thank Him for being in control, even when our situations seem completely out of control.

Life isn't always easy. Neither is always being thankful in all things, but that is God's will for every man who belongs to Jesus. And because it's God's will, He will help us maintain a heart of gratitude.

Pray:

Lord Jesus, when I face difficulty or suffering in this life, please remind me that it is Your will that I always maintain a heart attitude of thankfulness.

Walking the Walk

Read Proverbs 20:1–10

Key Verse:

The righteous lead blameless lives;
blessed are their children after them.
PROVERBS 20:7 NIV

Understand:

- Whom does Proverbs 20:7 refer to as "the righteous"?
- What do you think it means to live a "blameless life"? Do you think it's possible to live blamelessly in this life?

Apply:

Like it or not, your profession of faith in Jesus Christ is sure to put you under a microscope. Whether they are pulling for you to live a victorious life in Christ or they want to see you flounder, you can be sure that people will be watching you to see if your life—your words, your attitudes, and your actions—matches up with who you say you are in Christ.

This is why it's so important that each of us ask ourselves, *I talk the talk, but do I walk the walk?*

How your professed relationship with the Lord affects your attitude, speech, and actions truly matters.

An authentic walk with God can be a blessing to those in your sphere of influence—your friends, your coworkers, your business associates. . .and your family. On the other hand, an inauthentic walk can be a stumbling block to those who need to see what Jesus can do in a man's life.

Whether or not you walk closely with the Lord doesn't affect just you. And if you want to bless the people God has placed in your life, you'll be even more motivated to follow Jesus closely, to make Him your first priority, and to "live the same kind of life Christ lived" (1 John 2:6 NLV).

That's the kind of influence God calls you to have. . .at work, in your church, and in your home.

Pray:

Lord, I want to walk the walk and not just talk the talk when it comes to my life of faith. I know that my family, my friends, and others are watching, and I want them to see a reflection of You in everything I do and say.

Living by a "New" Law

Read John 13:31-35

Key Verse:

"I give you a new Law. You are to love each other. You must love each other as I have loved you."
John 13:34 NLV

Understand:

- Why is it important that you perform acts of love for other believers?
- In what ways can you best love and serve your brothers and sisters in Christ?

Apply:

Not long before He was arrested, tried, and crucified, Jesus taught His disciples what they should do so that people would know that they were His followers. It was this simple but all-important command: "Love each other. Just as I have loved you. . ." (John 13:34 NLT).

Jesus had just demonstrated His servant heart and His love for His disciples in the humblest of ways: by washing their feet (see John 13:1–17). In those days, only the lowliest of house servants were charged with washing the feet of the master's guests. Yet Jesus demonstrated His love and humility in this lowly way.

Now, after sending His betrayer, Judas, away to

commit a horrific sin against Him, Jesus gave them this "new" commandment. He had taught the disciples much about loving others and about loving God. But this commandment was different. The disciples, Jesus said, were to love one another "as I have loved you." Jesus had just spent three years loving the disciples—sacrificially, humbly, honestly—and He wanted them to know how important it was that they love one another the same way.

Jesus' words made a lasting impression on the disciple John, one of His closest followers, as they should on us. Decades later, the apostle wrote, "Dear friends, let us love one another, for love comes from God" (1 John 4:7 NIV).

So love others from your heart, especially your brothers and sisters in Christ.

Pray:

Lord Jesus, help me to love fellow believers the way You have loved me. Help me to always serve others from a heart of godly love.

Your Helper

Read John 14:15-26

Key Verse:

"But when the Father sends the Advocate as my representative—that is, the Holy Spirit—he will teach you everything and will remind you of everything I have told you."

JOHN 14:26 NLT

Understand:

- Why do you think Jesus referred to the Holy Spirit as "the Advocate"?
- What role does the Holy Spirit play in your life of faith today?

Apply:

Jesus had told His beloved disciples that He would be leaving them soon, and they likely felt a tidal wave of uncertainty wash over them. *What will we do when He's gone?* they probably wondered. *Are these past three years just going to waste?*

The disciples hadn't fully grasped Jesus' plan or purpose, so they didn't understand exactly why His time on earth with them had to come to an end. Jesus had known from the very beginning that He would be returning to His Father in heaven, leaving the disciples behind to continue the work He had started.

But Jesus wasn't leaving His servants to struggle through life on their own. That's why He promised them that He was going to ask God the Father to send them a helper—the Holy Spirit—to be with them when He was gone.

In this study's key verse, Jesus explained to the disciples that the Holy Spirit would be their teacher and would bring to their minds everything He had taught them during the past three years.

That was amazing news two thousand years ago, and it still is even now, for the same Holy Spirit who would take up residence in the disciples' hearts lives inside each of us who trust and follow Jesus today!

Pray:

Thank You, Jesus, that the Father has sent His Holy Spirit to live in my heart, teaching me the truth of the written Word, giving me strength, and guiding me in the way You want me to go.

Repelling the Devil

Read Matthew 4:1-11

Key Verse:

Jesus answered, "It is written: 'Man shall not live on bread alone, but on every word that comes from the mouth of God.'"

MATTHEW 4:4 NIV

Understand:

- In what ways do you think Satan tries to tempt you?
- How can you be ready when the devil tries to tempt or discourage you?

Apply:

In 1 Peter 5:8 (NIV), the apostle warned his readers, "Be alert and of sober mind. Your enemy the devil prowls around like a roaring lion looking for someone to devour."

Satan is indeed the enemy of your very soul, and he works tirelessly to exploit your weaknesses so that he may "devour" you. He even attempted to bring Jesus down and short-circuit His mission here on earth.

The devil no doubt believed that he had Jesus right where he wanted Him. Jesus hadn't eaten in forty days, and His body was in desperate need of nourishment.

So the devil sidled up to Him and suggested that He turn some stones into bread. But Jesus refused, because He had come to serve others, not Himself, and turning stones to bread was not part of God's plan.

The devil tempted Jesus three times, and each time Jesus responded by wielding what Paul called "the sword of the Spirit," a.k.a. the Word of God (Ephesians 6:17). In doing that, He set an example we can all follow when the roaring lion attempts to devour us. Rather than argue with the devil, Jesus simply answered, "It is written. . ."

We too can resist the devil's tactics by answering his lies with the truth of God's Word.

Pray:

Thank You, Jesus, for showing me how I can resist the devil when he attempts to bring me down. Thank You for the Word of God, which the devil has no answer for.

Giving Up Self

Read Mark 8:34-38

Key Verses:

"If anyone wants to be My follower, he must give up himself and his own desires. He must take up his cross and follow Me. If anyone wants to keep his own life safe, he will lose it. If anyone gives up his life because of Me and because of the Good News, he will save it."

MARK 8:34–35 NLV

Understand:

- What does it mean to you to be a follower of Jesus?
- What does it mean to take up your cross each day?

Apply:

In John 10:10 (NIV), Jesus told His followers, "I have come that they may have life, and have it to the full." That's a great promise to the one who chooses to follow Jesus without reservation, the one who would "give up himself and his own desires."

In today's key verses, Jesus called those who would follow Him to a deep, radical commitment to Him and His desires for them, even in the face of difficulties and opposition. This isn't a temporary sacrifice but a complete and permanent giving up of one's own will and desires for His sake and for His purposes.

As Christian men, we all desire to live the full life Jesus promised. But that means that we, the selfish creatures we are, must let go of our own desires and instead pursue God's plan for our lives.

It's a struggle we must engage in daily, and this world—as well as our own desires—will most certainly place obstacles in our path. But giving up everything daily is the best choice we can make because it's the choice that leads to the truly abundant life.

Pray:

Lord Jesus, You made it clear that following You means giving up my own desires in favor of Yours. I have a selfish side, so I need Your help. Show me how following You as You've instructed leads me to a truly full life.

The Key to Greatness

Read Matthew 20:20-28

Key Verses:

"Whoever wants to become great among you must be your servant, and whoever wants to be first must be your slave."
MATTHEW 20:26–27 NIV

Understand:

- What does it mean to you to be a servant or a slave?
- Why is it often difficult to serve the way Jesus did?

Apply:

The mother of the disciples James and John inadvertently stirred up a hornets' nest of dissension with the other ten when she approached Jesus and asked Him to grant her sons special places in His coming kingdom. She obviously had no idea what she was asking, but that didn't keep the other disciples from feeling more than a little piqued over what had happened.

Jesus, as He often did, used this earthly conflict to teach His followers a heavenly truth. After talking about the *wrong* way to achieve greatness, He spoke of the *right* way when He said, "Whoever wants to become great among you must be your servant, and whoever wants to be first must be your slave."

Being a servant and a slave to others doesn't mean engaging in false humility or allowing others to take advantage of you. It means that your life is marked by consistently treating others as though they are more important than you are. It means putting them and their needs ahead of your own.

In short, it means serving others the way Jesus did while He was here on earth.

Do you want to be great in God's kingdom? Then always make it your goal to humbly put others ahead of yourself and to joyfully serve those who can benefit from your service.

Pray:

Lord Jesus, help me to always remember that You want me to put others ahead of myself and care for others every day.

Thankful Offerings

Read Psalm 50:7-15

Key Verses:

"Sacrifice thank offerings to God, fulfill your vows to the Most High, and call on me in the day of trouble; I will deliver you, and you will honor me."

PSALM 50:14–15 NIV

Understand:

- For what are you most thankful today?
- How can you express your gratitude each day?

Apply:

In Old Testament times, God's people lived under a system of animal sacrifices that atoned for their sins. It wasn't a perfect system as it needed to be repeated periodically. It was, in fact, a foreshadowing of what was to come, namely the once-and-for-all sacrifice of Jesus Christ on a wooden cross.

Today's study is based on an Old Testament–era writing by a man named Asaph, and it describes a different kind of sacrifice, one that is at its heart deeply relational and that costs us nothing other than opening our mouths and hearts and speaking words of thanksgiving to the one who has given us everything.

God's Word repeatedly encourages all men to express gratitude to the Lord. For example, Paul wrote, "Rejoice always, pray continually, *give thanks in all circumstances*; for this is God's will for you in Christ Jesus" (1 Thessalonians 5:16–18 NIV, italics added).

It's easy to speak words of gratitude when life is going well. But what about when illness, financial distress, or broken relationships make their way into our world? Those are the times when Paul's words *in all circumstances* apply.

When you have a relationship with God through the Lord Jesus Christ, He gives you a perspective radically different from those who don't know Him. When you have Jesus, you truly have everything. For that reason, you can be truly thankful in *all* circumstances.

Pray:

Lord Jesus, I am so thankful for all You've done for me and all You are to me. May I never neglect expressing my gratitude each day.

Purity of Heart

Read Matthew 5:27-32

Key Verse:

"But I tell you that anyone who looks at a woman lustfully has already committed adultery with her in his heart."
MATTHEW 5:28 NIV

Understand:

- Do you find it difficult to keep your eyes from dwelling on what is impure? How can you do better in that area?
- How can you guard your heart from impurity?

Apply:

In this study's scripture passage, Jesus began His main point by quoting God's seventh commandment: "You shall not commit adultery" (Exodus 20:14 NIV). In Old Testament times, God had forbidden sexual activity outside marriage, and that commandment still stands today. But Jesus took this prohibition to a different level, teaching that it isn't just about where we take our bodies but also (even more importantly) about the impure places our hearts and minds can so easily go.

Jesus wanted those listening to His Sermon on

the Mount to understand that sin was a matter of the heart, not just a matter of their actions. He understood, and wanted them to understand, the importance of guarding their hearts by guarding their eyes.

Avoiding lust in today's sex-saturated world is no easy task. Sometimes it seems as though every other image that comes across our field of vision has the potential to cause us problems. Making things even more difficult is the fact that we men tend to be very visually oriented, meaning that our eyes are drawn to things that give us pleasure, especially sinful pleasure.

No, it's not an easy task, keeping our hearts and minds free from lust and our eyes off the things that cause us to stray. For us men today, it's a matter of commitment. . .to our wives, to our children, and to our faith.

Pray:

Dear Jesus, help me to keep my heart pure from lust and my eyes away from those things that take my mind to impure places.

Mountain-Moving Faith

Read Matthew 21:18-22

Key Verses:

"I tell you the truth, if you have faith and don't doubt, you can do things like this and much more. You can even say to this mountain, 'May you be lifted up and thrown into the sea,' and it will happen. You can pray for anything, and if you have faith, you will receive it."

MATTHEW 21:21–22 NLT

Understand:

- What things do you know that God wants you to believe Him for today?
- How can you overcome your doubts and build mountain-moving faith?

Apply:

Early one morning, Jesus was hungry, so He approached a green, leafy fig tree to pick some tasty figs for breakfast. But when He stood before the tree and found that it was bearing no fruit, He cursed it and it quickly wilted and died.

Jesus' disciples looked with astonishment at a withered fig tree that had recently been a lush, beautiful plant. "How did it die so quickly?" they asked Him, and Jesus explained that this unusual miracle was the result of His prayer of faith that the tree would no longer bear fruit. He then encouraged them to have that same kind of faith.

This account shows us two things about prayer: First, it must be offered in faith, and second, it must be in agreement with God's will. When Jesus cursed the fig tree, He knew it would die. He also knew that it was His Father's will that He use the dead fig tree to teach His disciples an important lesson about the relationship between faith and answered prayer.

Pray:

Jesus, thank You for teaching Your disciples, including me, the importance of faith when we pray. Help me to develop the mountain-moving faith You taught about.

Light of the World

Read John 8:12-20

Key Verse:

Again Jesus spoke to them, saying, "I am the light of the world. Whoever follows me will not walk in darkness, but will have the light of life."
John 8:12 ESV

Understand:

- What does it mean to you that Jesus Christ is "the light of the world"?
- How can you best walk in Jesus' light?

Apply:

You don't have to look long or far to see that this fallen world is shrouded in terrible spiritual death and darkness. Tragically, sin, violence, brokenness, and lostness are the rules and not the exceptions for human existence here on earth. This overwhelming darkness affects each of us on a deeply individual level. Men have no hope of getting themselves on the track God intended for them. No hope, that is, but Jesus!

In this study's key verse, Jesus self-identified as "the light of the world," meaning He is the one and only source of spiritual light. Jesus wanted His listeners, including us today, to understand that they didn't have to live lives filled with hopelessness, darkness, and slavery to sin. On the contrary, they could live in His light if they would simply believe in and faithfully follow Him. To this day, Jesus gives those who follow Him the transforming, revitalizing "light of life."

Decades after Jesus had returned to heaven, the apostle John wrote, "If we walk in the light, as he is in the light. . .the blood of Jesus, his Son, purifies us from all sin" (1 John 1:7 NIV). What a comforting, transforming promise!

There's no way around it—you live in a dark, lost world. But Jesus has promised to give you light, a light that overcomes all the world's darkness.

Pray:

Thank You, Jesus, that I can walk in Your light every minute of every day.

The Bread of Life

Read John 6:32-40

Key Verse:

Then Jesus declared, "I am the bread of life.
Whoever comes to me will never go hungry,
and whoever believes in me will never be thirsty."
John 6:35 niv

Understand:

- How does Jesus provide spiritual nourishment to those starving for His life?
- Can you think of two or three people you know who need to partake of the bread of life?

Apply:

We live in a world filled with the spiritually hungry and thirsty—those who need to partake of Jesus, the Savior who alone can satisfy them so that they never hunger or thirst again.

Speaking to a big crowd gathered on the shoreline of the Sea of Galilee, Jesus spoke this promise: "Blessed are those who hunger and thirst for righteousness, for they will be filled" (Matthew 5:6 niv).

Jesus had come to earth to minister to spiritually hungry and thirsty people, and in today's key verse, He identified Himself as "the bread of life," meaning that He alone was the one who could provide the spiritual nourishment and hydration each man so desperately needs.

The people following Jesus when He pronounced His blessing on the spiritually hungry and thirsty knew that God had provided their ancestors with manna to keep them from starving in the desert. Every one of those ancestors eventually died, but Jesus told His listeners, "But here is the bread that comes down from heaven, which anyone may eat and not die" (John 6:50 NIV).

When you feel spiritually hungry and thirsty, run to Jesus. And when you encounter a man who is starving spiritually, point him to Jesus, who has promised everlasting satisfaction.

Pray:

Dear Jesus, only You can satisfy a man's spiritual hunger and thirst. May I encourage the hungry to turn to You alone for satisfaction.

It's About the Love!

Read Mark 12:28–34

Key Verses:

"'Love the Lord your God with all your heart and with all your soul and with all your mind and with all your strength.' The second is this: 'Love your neighbor as yourself.' There is no commandment greater than these."

Mark 12:30–31 NIV

Understand:

- In what ways can you best express your love for God?
- In what practical ways can you love your neighbor as yourself?

Apply:

The Jewish religious leaders in Jesus' day tried many times to bait Him into saying something incriminating so that they could arrest Him. One day, a religious teacher asked Jesus which Old Testament law was most important, probably believing that he had the Lord right where he wanted Him. But Jesus had the perfect answer, quoting Deuteronomy 6:5 (NIV), which says, "Love the Lord your God with all your heart and with all your soul and with all your strength," and Leviticus 19:18 (NIV), which tells us to "love your neighbor as yourself."

Love God and love your neighbors. Jesus' answer stunned the religious teacher, who could do nothing but agree with what He had just said. It really is that simple! And it's what should mark the life of every Christian man.

On a practical level, loving God means living a life of holiness, devotion, worship, and gratitude for all He has done for you. Loving your neighbor as yourself means treating people with kindness, patience, and hospitality, showing respect and civility to those you disagree with, and making a life goal to help meet other people's needs.

Loving Jesus and your neighbor from your heart helps others, and it puts you in a position to receive His very best for you.

Pray:

Jesus, I want others to see You in me, so help me to obey what You called the greatest commandments. Empower me to love You and my neighbors from my heart and in my actions.

Broken

Read Psalm 51:10-19

Key Verses:

You do not desire a sacrifice, or I would offer one. You do not want a burnt offering. The sacrifice you desire is a broken spirit. You will not reject a broken and repentant heart, O God.

Psalm 51:16–17 NLT

Understand:

- What did David plead with God to do for him in Psalm 51?
- When did you last feel truly broken over some sin in your life?

Apply:

David was heartbroken and filled with sorrow when he wrote Psalm 51. The prophet Nathan had confronted the king for his terrible sin of committing adultery with Bathsheba, the wife of Uriah, one of David's finest, most devoted warriors. Worse yet, when David discovered that Bathsheba was pregnant with his child, he arranged for Uriah to be killed in battle, making him both an adulterer and a murderer.

Nathan had let David know that he would face the consequences for his sin, but in Psalm 51, David's focus was not on what he would suffer for his wrongdoing but on the damage he had done to his relationship with God.

David could have offered sacrifices and burnt offerings, but he understood that God was looking for a broken spirit and a repentant heart—just as He does with us today.

Brokenness and regret for our sin never feel good—in fact, they can feel awful. But these things lead us to confession and repentance, which is the key to restoration with the Lord. And when we confess our sins, "he is faithful and just and will forgive us our sins and purify us from all unrighteousness" (1 John 1:9 NIV).

Pray:

Lord, give me a broken spirit and a repentant heart when I sin against You. Keep me sensitive to Your Holy Spirit so that I can hear Him when He convicts me of sin.

The Fear of the Lord

Read Acts 9:19-31

Key Verse:

Then the church throughout Judea, Galilee and Samaria enjoyed a time of peace and was strengthened. Living in the fear of the Lord and encouraged by the Holy Spirit, it increased in numbers.

Acts 9:31 NIV

Understand:

- What does it mean to you to fear the Lord?
- How can you best cultivate in your heart a fitting reverence for God?

Apply:

Today, we don't hear of someone being a "God-fearing man" nearly as often as we used to. But the key verse in today's study says that the fledgling first-century church lived "in the fear of the Lord" and were "encouraged by the Holy Spirit."

What a fitting description for a healthy, growing congregation of believers—and for an individual follower of Jesus Christ as well!

Throughout the pages of scripture, we read of many godly men who were said to have "feared the Lord."

These men didn't fear God in the sense that they were scared of Him and wanted to hide from Him. Rather, they understood that God wasn't just their Creator but also their loving Father. They had walked with Him closely enough that they stood in awe of His holiness, greatness, and majesty.

The Bible says, "The fear of the Lord is the beginning of wisdom" (Proverbs 9:10 NIV), but it also says, "Let us then approach God's throne of grace with confidence, so that we may receive mercy and find grace to help us in our time of need" (Hebrews 4:16 NIV).

The Christian man has the amazing privilege even today to approach God's throne of grace with boldness and confidence, not in fear and trembling. But we must approach Him bringing with us the sense of awe He fully deserves.

Pray:

Father in heaven, may I never lose my sense of awe or reverent fear over Your holiness, greatness, and majesty. . .or over Your great love for me.

Keep Watching, Keep Praying

Read Mark 14:32-42

Key Verses:

Then he returned and found the disciples asleep. He said to Peter, "Simon, are you asleep? Couldn't you watch with me even one hour? Keep watch and pray, so that you will not give in to temptation. For the spirit is willing, but the body is weak."

MARK 14:37–38 NLT

Understand:

- What does it mean to you to watch and pray?
- How does knowing that your flesh is weak motivate you to pray?

Apply:

The apostle Peter once issued his readers this sobering warning: "Stay alert! Watch out for your great enemy, the devil. He prowls around like a roaring lion, looking for someone to devour" (1 Peter 5:8 NLT).

It probably isn't a stretch to say that Peter learned a little something about the devil's tactics through a very difficult personal experience. The night before Jesus' crucifixion, He took Peter, James, and John with Him to the garden of Gethsemane, where He separated Himself from His friends and prayed a wrenching prayer to the Father asking for a way out of the suffering He was about to endure on behalf of sinful, lost humanity. Jesus' divine side was willing; His human side wanted a way out.

When Jesus returned to His disciples, He found them sleeping, and He exhorted Peter to "watch and pray so that you will not fall into temptation. The spirit is willing, but the flesh is weak" (Mark 14:38 NIV). Indeed, Peter's flesh proved to be weak, as he first abandoned Jesus and later denied even knowing Him (see Mark 14:66–72).

Jesus understood that the disciples' flesh was prone to failing them, and He knows the same thing about us today. That is why He speaks the same message to His followers today: Watch and pray.

Pray:

Lord Jesus, I know my flesh is weak. Help me to always be alert to temptation and to rely on You for strength.

Proclaiming God's Wonderful Name

Read Psalm 105:1-11

Key Verses:

Give praise to the LORD, proclaim his name; make known among the nations what he has done. Sing to him, sing praise to him; tell of all his wonderful acts.

PSALM 105:1–2 NIV

Understand:

- What great things has God done in and for you? How do you respond to those things?
- How can you make praising the Lord a more regular part of your life of faith?

Apply:

Each follower of Christ has a testimony, a story to tell about how he first came to faith in Jesus. Some of us grew up in Christian homes and remained in the faith as adults. Others of us were saved out of rough backgrounds of rebellion, immorality, addiction, and other types of sin. No matter where your story fits in, you are still the beneficiary of God's great love, compassion, and kindness, and He wants you to speak words of thanksgiving and praise for the amazing things He has done for you.

Psalm 105 opens with the encouragement to "give praise to the Lord" and continues with inspirational urgings to proclaim His name, to let the nations know of what He has done, and to speak of His wonderful acts.

The Bible enjoins God's people to proclaim His name and to celebrate all the wonders He has done. For the Christian man, this starts with salvation and the amazing truth that God has done something no man could do for himself and continues His transforming work every day.

Your testimony is a proclamation of what God alone can do. So open your mouth and "tell of all his wonderful acts."

Pray:

Thank You, Jesus, for doing for me what I could never do for myself. May I openly proclaim Your goodness and miraculous works whenever You give me the opportunity.

Shining Your Light

Read Matthew 5:11–16

Key Verse:

"In the same way, let your light shine before others, that they may see your good deeds and glorify your Father in heaven."
MATTHEW 5:16 NIV

Understand:

- What does it mean to you to let your light shine in this dark world?
- How can you let your light shine better every day?

Apply:

When you first came to Jesus in saving faith, He didn't just snatch you up and take you to heaven (that comes later!). No, He left you here on earth and gave you an important assignment, which He stated clearly in this study's key verse.

"Let your light shine before others." This means purposefully letting your thoughts, your attitudes, and your actions reflect the light (Christ) every day and in every way. It means living a life that tells others about Jesus before you even speak a word. It means living in such a way that others see Jesus in you and think well of Him.

Jesus is the true light of the world (John 8:12), and when we come to Him in faith, when we abide in Him and make obedience to Him our top priority, He fills us with His Spirit so that we can grow in Him and become more and more like Him every day. When that happens, His light shines from inside us out into the world, which leads to glory for our loving Father in heaven. That's your main purpose while you're still here on earth.

Are you letting your light shine before others every day?

Pray:

Jesus, You are the light of the world. I want Your light to shine from deep within me out into the world so that God will be glorified. Thank You for allowing me and empowering me to shine for You.

Receiving God's Best

Read Numbers 13:25-33

Key Verses:

But the men who had gone up with [Caleb] said, "We can't attack those people; they are stronger than we are." And they spread among the Israelites a bad report about the land they had explored.

Numbers 13:31–32 NIV

Understand:

- What kinds of obstacles cause your faith to falter and prevent you from receiving what God has for you?
- How can you stay focused on God's promises and not on the "giants" that stand in your way?

Apply:

The people of Israel were gathered at the border of the land God had promised to give them. Imagine the excited buzz going through their ranks as they thought about finally receiving the land of promise!

But there was a problem—a *big* problem.

Moses had sent twelve spies to scope out the land. After the spies returned to the Israelites, they all agreed that it was everything they could have hoped for. But ten of the spies focused on the challenges of taking the land—specifically the giants who lived there—and began spreading fear among the people.

All this led to a rebellion among the people, who complained to Moses that trying to take the land would lead to disaster. God, angered at their lack of faith, barred these unbelieving people from taking the Promised Land for another forty years.

In Matthew 17:20 (NIV), Jesus spoke of the power of properly placed faith: "Truly I tell you, if you have faith as small as a mustard seed, you can say to this mountain, 'Move from here to there,' and it will move. Nothing will be impossible for you."

God always keeps His promises, and we should never make the tragic mistake of focusing on the "giants" before us instead of on our even bigger God.

Pray:

Lord, may I always focus on You and not on the potential obstacles before me.

Clothing Yourself with Jesus

Read Romans 13:8–14

Key Verse:

Clothe yourself with the presence of the Lord Jesus Christ. And don't let yourself think about ways to indulge your evil desires.

Romans 13:14 NLT

Understand:

- What, according to this study's scripture reading, fulfills the law?
- What "deeds of darkness" (Romans 13:12 NIV) does Paul say we are to avoid?

Apply:

One of the first things many of us notice about a man is what he's wearing. And while we shouldn't judge a guy based on how he's dressed, a man will do well to make sure he is dressed appropriately for specific social or business situations. For example, it wouldn't be wise to wear cargo shorts and a Boston Red Sox jersey to a job interview.

The apostle Paul used clothing in a figurative way in Romans 13:14 when he wrote, "Clothe yourself with the presence of the Lord Jesus Christ." That's a word picture that describes how a man can show the world around him the goodness, the glory, and the work of Jesus in his life.

Jesus should be our spiritual clothing—and when He is, we will focus on representing Him well and not on satisfying our own desires. We'll avoid what Paul called "deeds of darkness" and behave and speak in a manner fitting a child of the living God. When we do that, people will notice, and they will know that we belong to Jesus.

When you get up in the morning, it's important that you dress appropriately for what you'll be doing that day. But it's far more important that you clothe yourself in Jesus!

Pray:

Lord Jesus, may I cover myself in Your wonderful presence each and every moment of each and every day so that I live in a way that pleases and glorifies You.

Wisdom from Above

Read James 1:2–11

Key Verses:

If any of you lacks wisdom, you should ask God, who gives generously to all without finding fault, and it will be given to you. But when you ask, you must believe and not doubt, because the one who doubts is like a wave of the sea, blown and tossed by the wind.

James 1:5–6 NIV

Understand:

- How do you define wisdom, and why do you think you need it?
- What do you think you should do when you need answers to a sticky life question?

Apply:

When you're faced with an overwhelming problem or if you just need some answers concerning work or ministry, you're going to need some wisdom. Wisdom keeps men from bad decisions and leads them to choices that benefit themselves and glorify the Lord.

If we're honest with ourselves, most of us would have to admit that we could use more wisdom as we navigate our way through life. The good news is that the Bible promises to give us all the wisdom we need, provided we ask for it in faith. When we confidently ask God for the wisdom we need, "He is always ready to give it to [us]" (James 1:5 NLV).

The apostle James also used an amazing description of the wisdom God gives those who request it. Godly wisdom, according to James 3:17 (NIV), is "pure; then peace-loving, considerate, submissive, full of mercy and good fruit, impartial and sincere."

Without God's wisdom, we aren't capable of being the kind of men, the kind of leaders, and the kinds of husbands and fathers He's called us to be. But *with* His wisdom, we can be all those things and more.

Pray:

Lord God, I need Your perfect brand of wisdom so that I can overcome when life gets rough and try to make a difference in this lost and hurting world.

The Shepherd's Voice

Read John 10:22-30

Key Verses:

"My sheep listen to my voice; I know them, and they follow me. I give them eternal life, and they shall never perish; no one will snatch them out of my hand. My Father, who has given them to me, is greater than all; no one can snatch them out of my Father's hand."

JOHN 10:27–29 NIV

Understand:

- In what ways do you see yourself as one of Jesus' sheep?
- In what specific ways can you make sure you are hearing and listening to Jesus' voice daily?

Apply:

If you know anything about sheep, you probably understand that they are among the world's most dependent creatures. Sheep need nourishment, water, and protection—all things the shepherd or farmer provides. Domesticated sheep just can't last long without this provision. Because the shepherd provides the things needed, the sheep quickly learn to follow when they hear his voice.

On a few occasions, Jesus likened His followers to sheep and called Himself their shepherd. Jesus cares for His sheep in many ways, and in this study's key verses, He spoke of His sheep listening for His voice and choosing to follow Him.

Just as sheep can't last long without hearing their shepherd's voice, we followers of Christ need to hear Jesus' voice if we are to grow and thrive in our relationship with Him. We first heard Jesus when we began our lives in Him; as time goes on, we become more familiar with His voice as we spend time reading scripture and praying and allowing the Holy Spirit to work within us. And as we hear His voice, we learn to follow Him more and more closely each day.

Pray:

Jesus, I thank You that I have heard Your voice—and can continue consistently hearing Your voice so that I can always follow You.

Life in the Spirit

Read Galatians 5:16-26

Key Verses:

But the fruit of the Spirit is love, joy, peace, forbearance, kindness, goodness, faithfulness, gentleness and self-control. Against such things there is no law.

Galatians 5:22–23 NIV

Understand:

- In what way did Paul enjoin believers to "walk" in this passage?
- How do acts of the flesh contrast with the fruit of the Spirit?

Apply:

In Galatians 5, Paul offered a stark contrast between a life lived in the flesh and a life lived in the Spirit. A life lived in the flesh produces a long list of sinful actions and attitudes that lead to eternal destruction.

A life lived in the Spirit, on the other hand, will produce the fruit of the Spirit: "love, joy, peace, forbearance, kindness, goodness, faithfulness, gentleness and self-control"—all qualities that lead a man to live the right kind of life, which in turn leads to God's blessings.

Any fruit farmer knows that he can't just stick a sapling in the ground and expect a yield of quality fruit.

No, in order for a tree to produce the optimal harvest of high-quality fruit, it must be fed, watered, and pruned regularly. When he does those things faithfully, his trees will produce delicious fruit that will bring him the highest profit.

Paul likened us believers to fruit trees, and that means we must be fed and watered—and, yes, pruned from time to time—if we are to grow in our faith, become progressively more like Jesus, and produce the very best fruit for God's eternal kingdom.

Pray:

Lord Jesus, I want my life to demonstrate what the presence of Your Holy Spirit can do. There is much room for growth in me, so I yield myself to You so that I can become more and more like You each day.

Being a "Doer"

Read James 1:19-27

Key Verse:

Do not merely listen to the word,
and so deceive yourselves. Do what it says.
JAMES 1:22 NIV

Understand:

- What is your plan of action to read, study, and memorize the Word of God?
- How can you become more obedient to the commands in scripture?

Apply:

If a man goes to his physician for his annual physical examination and the doctor finds that he's twenty pounds overweight and his blood pressure is high, then advises the patient to get more exercise, lay off the fried fatty foods and sugary drinks, and lose twenty, what would be his best course of action? Obviously, he'd heed his doctor's advice and come up with a plan of action to get in better shape. Otherwise. . .

That's very much how the Word of God should function in the life of the believer, according to this study's key verse.

In 2 Timothy 3:16–17 (NIV), the apostle Paul

wrote, "All Scripture is God-breathed and is useful for teaching, rebuking, correcting and training in righteousness, so that the servant of God may be thoroughly equipped for every good work."

Those are some great benefits, aren't they? But no matter how much a man reads, studies, or memorizes the Bible, he'll never reap any of them if he doesn't heed the Word and do what it says.

James' message might seem a little bit obvious, but it's still a great reminder for any believer to put the Word of God into practice in his life each and every day. When we do that, we put ourselves in a position to be the kind of men God has created us to be.

Pray:

Dear Jesus, thank You for giving me the written Word. May I always heed and obey what it says I must do. May I never neglect to be a true doer of what I read in scripture.

Desperation. . .and Faith

Read 1 Chronicles 5:11–22

Key Verse:

They were helped in fighting them, and God delivered the Hagrites and all their allies into their hands, because they cried out to him during the battle. He answered their prayers, because they trusted in him.

1 Chronicles 5:20 NIV

Understand:

- When was the last time you had to cry out to God in desperation?
- What condition did the people in the above passage meet in order for God to miraculously intervene on their behalf?

Apply:

Sometimes we find ourselves in situations so desperate that all we can do is cry out to God for help. The reading for this study tells the story of the Reubenites, the Gadites, and the half tribe of Manasseh, three tribes battling with a people called the Hagrites. In the midst of the battle, the tribes did two things that helped them to emerge victorious: They cried out to God *and* they trusted in Him.

The three tribes knew that if God didn't come through, they were sunk. But they also knew that their God was more than big enough to give them victory.

That's what faith is all about!

Today, thousands of years after the battle recounted in 1 Chronicles 5, we serve the same mighty God, and He still responds positively to our faith. What's more, we have this promise straight from the mouth of Jesus: "And I will do whatever you ask in my name, so that the Father may be glorified in the Son" (John 14:13 NIV).

When we're going through a particularly difficult life battle, when we're in desperate need of help, we have a God we can trust to step up on our behalf. Our part in that bargain is that we present our pleas to Him, believing that He *can* and *will* give us the help we need.

Pray:

Lord Jesus, when I'm in the midst of battle in this life, remind me that You are with me and willing and more than able to intervene on my behalf in even the direst of situations.

Just Praise Him!

Read Psalm 47:1-7

Key Verses:

Sing praises to God, sing praises; sing praises to our King, sing praises. For God is the King of all the earth; sing to him a psalm of praise.

PSALM 47:6–7 NIV

Understand:

- How can you best incorporate praise into your daily times of prayer?
- Why do you think God likes it when we speak or sing words of praise to Him?

Apply:

Someone once suggested that God likes it when His people praise Him, not because He's vain or needs our affirmation but because He wants to bless us and more intimately share Himself with the objects of His love.

The psalms are filled with encouragements to lift our voices and praise God. In today's key verses, we are encouraged no fewer than five times to sing praises to Him!

But the psalms aren't the only place in the Bible that encourages believers to praise God. In the New Testament, the apostle Paul enjoined Christians to "be filled with the Spirit, speaking to one another with psalms, hymns, and songs from the Spirit. Sing and make music from your heart to the Lord, always giving thanks to God the Father for everything, in the name of our Lord Jesus Christ" (Ephesians 5:18–20 NIV).

Clearly, God likes it when we praise Him from our hearts!

So even if you don't think you can carry a tune, sing praises to God every chance you get. And if you don't sing, open your heart and your mouth and speak words of praise to the Lord. In your car, on the way to work, on the golf course. . .anywhere you can draw air, just open your heart, lift your voice, and praise the Lord!

Pray:

Loving heavenly Father, thank You for giving me my voice. May I never waste an opportunity to open my mouth and speak or sing words of praise to You.

Your Value to God

Read 1 Peter 1:13-21

Key Verses:

For you know that it was not with perishable things such as silver or gold that you were redeemed from the empty way of life handed down to you from your ancestors, but with the precious blood of Christ, a lamb without blemish or defect.

1 Peter 1:18–19 NIV

Understand:

- What does this study's passage mean when it says you are redeemed?
- In what ways did coming to faith in Jesus change how you now live?

Apply:

In today's scripture reading, the apostle Peter encouraged his readers toward lives far different from the ones they lived before they knew Jesus, for they had been redeemed through the blood of the Lord Jesus Christ.

Humanity was the crown jewel of God's creation, the only living thing He created in His image. When Adam and Eve chose to sin against God, they brought death and destruction to God's beloved creation. But the Lord, who still loved humanity as much as ever, had a plan to reconcile us to Himself.

God the Father demonstrated His love for us and our value to Him when He gave His very best to bring us into His eternal kingdom: His own Son, who willingly shed His precious blood to pay the penalty for our sin and rebellion.

God's love for His people is both very deep and very personal: "See what kind of love the Father has given to us, that we should be called children of God; and so we are" (1 John 3:1 ESV).

You are valuable to your heavenly Father, so valuable that He sent Jesus to earth to shed His blood for you.

Pray:

Lord Jesus, thank You for valuing me so much that You were willing to shed Your precious blood so that I could live forever with You in heaven.

God's Love for the Helpless

Read Romans 5:1–11

Key Verse:

When we were utterly helpless, Christ came at just the right time and died for us sinners.

Romans 5:6 NLT

Understand:

- How does the above scripture reading affect the way you approach life's suffering and difficulties?
- Is it difficult for you to think of yourself as "helpless"? Why or why not?

Apply:

As a man, you probably like being described with adjectives such as *strong*, *able*, *competent*, *noble*, and others. We men don't usually like to think of ourselves as helpless. We like to think that no matter how dire our circumstances, no matter what kind of a pickle we find ourselves in, we can pull ourselves up by our bootstraps and find a way to work things out.

The Bible, however, teaches that when it comes to our sin and its consequences, we are helpless—lost in the darkness of our sin and completely unable to find a way out. That's what Romans 5:6 means when it says that before we came to faith in Jesus, each of us was "utterly helpless."

But there is hope, a hope God Himself provided. Romans 5:6 also shows us the greatness of the love of God, who sent Jesus to die for ungodly people, people who in and of themselves are undeserving and unlovable, who can do nothing on their own about their lost and dying state.

What an amazing act of love and mercy!

When you think of how hopeless and helpless you are without Jesus, you can't help but praise God and thank Him for loving you so deeply that He gave the very best He had to offer.

Pray:

Jesus, I know that without You I am helpless and without hope. But You came at God's appointed time to die for me and rescue me from the consequences of my sin. Now, because of Your great mercy and love, I can live a life of confidence and of service for You.

A New Life Focus

Read Matthew 4:18–22

Key Verse:

And he said to them, "Follow me,
and I will make you fishers of men."
MATTHEW 4:19 ESV

Understand:

- What does it mean to you to follow Jesus?
- What does being a "fisher of men" mean to you today?

Apply:

Take a few minutes to think about how your focus, your goals, and your priorities changed after you began to follow Jesus. Where you were inwardly focused, concerned mainly with career, work, and your own goals and desires, you are now outwardly focused, concerned with those things having to do with God's eternal kingdom.

That's what happened to Simon Peter and his brother, Andrew.

At the very moment Jesus called these two fishermen to follow Him, He let them know that their life focus would be changing. Following Jesus often means leaving certain things behind to pursue something far grander, and in this case, Peter and Andrew would be leaving a life of fishing for a life of bringing others to Jesus.

Peter and Andrew left everything they had ever known to follow Jesus, and henceforth they would follow Jesus everywhere He went—witnessing His miracles and learning from Him. And when those three years of following and learning were over, they were ready to do the work He had called them to do when He first said to them, "Follow me."

Matthew's Gospel reports that Peter and Andrew immediately "left their nets and followed him" (4:20 NIV). In doing that, they set an example for all disciples of Christ: Follow Jesus, even when it means leaving behind the things that are most important to you.

Pray:

Jesus, I know You want me to be a "fisher of men," and that means following You and being laser focused on You. Remind me to follow You daily so that I may learn from You and grow in my relationship with You.

Give Thanks!

Read Psalm 106:1-2, 47-48

Key Verse:

Praise the L*ORD! Give thanks to the* L*ORD,*
for he is good! His faithful love endures forever.
Psalm 106:1 NLT

Understand:

- How can you cultivate an attitude of thankfulness?
- For what are you thankful to the Lord today?

Apply:

The Bible repeatedly encourages believers to speak words of thanksgiving to the Lord, regardless of our present circumstances. Whether you feel blessed or whether you feel stressed and needy. . .give thanks to the Lord.

Sometimes it's not so easy to feel thankful to the Lord. When life is hard, when your circumstances are far from ideal, it's easier to just keep your mouth shut and suffer in silence or to complain about your present situation.

Does that sound like you sometimes?

But the Bible states that we men of God should be grateful at all times and in all life situations. That's what Paul meant when he wrote, "Give thanks in all circumstances; for this is God's will for you in Christ Jesus" (1 Thessalonians 5:18 NIV).

God's will? You're probably letting out a sigh and wondering how you can possibly summon up a thankful attitude. You may even be thinking, *Can't God see what I'm going through right now?*

First of all, God does see what you're going through, and He cares. . .very deeply. Second, He's shown you how you can cultivate gratitude in your heart in today's key verse. Psalm 106, written by an unknown writer, declares, "Give thanks to the LORD, for he is good! His faithful love endures forever."

Even when you feel like nothing good is going on in your life, you can be thankful for the Lord Himself. He is good, and His love is both faithful and eternal.

Pray:

Lord Jesus, thank You for Your everlasting love and unfailing goodness.

Your Good Shepherd

Read John 10:7-18

Key Verse:

"I am the good shepherd. The good shepherd lays down his life for the sheep."

John 10:11 ESV

Understand:

- How is your relationship with God like that of a sheep to its shepherd?
- What benefits do you enjoy because Jesus is your good shepherd?

Apply:

People living in the land of Israel while Jesus was on earth, and well before that, understood the relationship between shepherds and sheep. They knew that shepherds had an important assignment: providing their sheep with protection, food, and water. If the shepherd failed in any of his duties, the sheep, being the nearly helpless domesticated creatures they were, stood little chance of surviving for long. Left on their own, they would either be carried away by hungry predators or die of hunger and thirst.

Centuries before Jesus came to earth, David wrote Psalm 23, which begins, "The Lord is my shepherd,

I lack nothing" (verse 1 NIV). When Jesus said, "I am the good shepherd," He identified Himself as the one David depended on for care, provision, and protection.

But Jesus took His role as our good shepherd an astonishing step further when He said, "The good shepherd lays down his life for the sheep." While it's extremely unlikely that an earthly shepherd would ever give up his life for his flock, Jesus did that very thing when He willingly went to the cross to die in the place of His sheep.

We all need Jesus' love and care and sacrifice. Without those things, we have no chance of surviving spiritually. With them, we can live victorious, fruitful lives of faith.

Pray:

Jesus, thank You for being my good shepherd. May I always trust You enough to follow You and to depend on You for safety, provision, and restoration for my soul.

Jesus: The Way and the Truth and the Life

Read John 14:5-14

Key Verse:

Jesus answered, "I am the way and the truth and the life. No one comes to the Father except through me."

John 14:6 niv

Understand:

- What does Jesus state about His true identity in today's reading?
- Would you describe the gospel message as "inclusive" or "exclusive"? Why?

Apply:

We live in a culture that prides itself on being inclusive, which means differing values, religious beliefs, and approaches to spirituality are esteemed and accepted as truth. "Whatever works for you is your own path and your own truth," we're told.

And most men believe that.

But the Bible makes it clear that there is but one way for us sinful humans to be at peace with a holy God.

In John 14:6, Jesus made perhaps His most definitive statement concerning who He really is and what it means for each of us today. Jesus was and is. . .

- *The Way:* Jesus is the only way to salvation. God has clearly communicated in His written Word that only one sacrifice is acceptable to Him for the forgiveness of sin: His one and only Son.
- *The Truth:* You've probably heard it said that each man needs to find his own truth. But Jesus stated clearly that He is God's truth itself.
- *The Life:* Jesus alone is the source of life—both life on this earth and eternal life in God's kingdom.

Jesus is the way and the truth and the life. And as His faithful followers, we must never shrink back from declaring the truth that no one comes to the Father except through Him.

Pray:

Thank You, Jesus, for being the way to peace with God and for being my source of eternal truth and life. May I never forget that when I tell others about You.

Our Source of Righteousness

Read Romans 3:21-31

Key Verse:

So we are made right with God through faith and not by obeying the law.
ROMANS 3:28 NLT

Understand:

- How does knowing that you are justified by God's free gift of grace help shape your attitude toward Him?
- What would you say to encourage a man who believed his sins were too terrible for God to forgive?

Apply:

The first two and a half chapters of the book of Romans are pretty much all bad news for fallen, sinful humanity. Paul made the point that all men—Jews and Gentiles alike—are sinners who have no hope of earning God's forgiveness or salvation from the terrible eternal consequences of their wrongdoing.

But in Romans 3, Paul made a radical change in focus. Yes, we are all lost in our sin, but there is good news ahead because God has lovingly and freely provided what only He can provide: righteousness and forgiveness for even the worst of our sins. Through Jesus' sacrificial death, we can be forgiven; through our faith in Him we can be redeemed and transformed into what we were not, and could never be, before.

The Bible teaches that before we came to Christ for salvation, each of us was completely spiritually dead because of our sins. But God's infinite love and compassion motivated Him to provide a way for the spiritually dead to have life. He did that when He sent His Son to die for us and then be raised from the dead so that we could be made alive in Him.

Never forget, your salvation has *nothing* to do with anything good in you and *everything* to do with God's goodness and love.

Pray:

Thank You, Jesus, that the Father in heaven loved me, a man who was dead in my sins, and brought me to life everlasting. That is what God's amazing grace is all about!

Facing Your Fear

Read Psalm 56:1-11

Key Verses:

In God, whose word I praise, in the Lord, whose word I praise—in God I trust and am not afraid. What can man do to me?
Psalm 56:10–11 NIV

Understand

- What things or situations cause you to feel fearful?
- What does it mean for you to "walk not according to the flesh but according to the Spirit" (Romans 8:4 SKJV)?

Apply:

David wrote Psalm 56 in a time of great fear, loneliness, and desperation. He had been on the run from the insanely jealous and hateful King Saul, who intended to murder him and eliminate the threat to his place on the throne. David ended up hiding out in a place called Gath.

While David no doubt felt the same emotions any man would when his life is in danger, he focused on his conviction that God was with him and for him (Psalm 56:9). This wasn't just David's hope or plea; it was his trust in what God had already said. In the end, David concluded, "What can man do to me?"

In today's world, very few men will ever face the kinds of threats David faced. That doesn't mean they won't face situations that leave them feeling fearful. But God is bigger than any*thing* or any*one* we could ever fear in this life. Not only that, this all-powerful, all-wise, all-loving God is unwaveringly *for* those of us He calls His children. And "if God is for us, who can be against us?" (Romans 8:31 NIV).

Knowing all this, what do you have to fear?

Pray:

Lord, I confess that I feel fearful at times.
Help me look past my fears and focus fully
on Your greatness and Your plans for me.
You are bigger than anything I could ever fear.

The Resurrection and the Life

Read John 11:20-27

Key Verses:

"I am the resurrection and the life. He who believes in Me, though he were dead, yet shall he live. And whoever lives and believes in Me shall never die."

JOHN 11:25–26 SKJV

Understand:

- What did Jesus mean when He said to Martha, "I am the resurrection and the life"?
- What does the story of Jesus raising Lazarus tell you about how He cares for those He loves?

Apply:

John 11:1–44 tells the wonderful story of Jesus miraculously raising His friend Lazarus from the dead. Jesus had known that Lazarus was deathly sick, but He waited two days before traveling to Bethany, Lazarus' hometown.

Jesus' disciples were confused as to why He waited to go to Bethany after receiving word of His friend's illness. But Jesus wasn't just waiting around for Lazarus to die. Jesus had a plan, one that led to God being glorified when He performed a miracle for Lazarus and his sisters, Mary and Martha.

As Jesus arrived in Bethany, Martha ran to Him to express her disappointment and grief—and her faith. Jesus knew what He was going to do that day. But first, He would teach Martha and Mary what could happen if only they believed.

Jesus stepped to the mouth of the tomb and called out, "Lazarus, come out!" (John 11:43 SKJV). Moments later, Lazarus stepped out of the darkness into the light of day. Jesus, the man who had just called Himself "the resurrection and the life," showed that death was no obstacle for Him.

Jesus is the one and only source of resurrection and eternal life. Without Him, we have neither, but with Him we will one day be raised from the dead and will have everlasting life.

Pray:

Jesus, remind me to always point to You as the source of everlasting life.

Fully Obedient

Read Numbers 27:12-23

Key Verses:

One day the Lord *said to Moses, "Climb one of the mountains east of the river, and look out over the land I have given the people of Israel. After you have seen it, you will die like your brother, Aaron, for you both rebelled against my instructions in the wilderness of Zin."*

Numbers 27:12–14 NLT

Understand:

- How important do you think it is to obey God fully and not partially?
- What does Moses' story teach you about finishing strong?

Apply:

God had called Moses to lead the Israelites out of Egyptian slavery. Moses would lead the people on their way to Canaan, also known as the Promised Land. Sadly, however, God barred Moses from completing his appointed mission and entering the land himself. That's because, in a moment of frustration, he failed to obey a simple command God had given him.

The Israelites had complained that they were thirsty,

so God told Moses to *speak* to a large rock, which would then miraculously send out a stream of water. But Moses *struck* the rock with his shepherd's staff instead—twice.

God still provided the water, but He told Moses, "Because you did not trust in me enough to honor me as holy in the sight of the Israelites, you will not bring this community into the land I give them" (Numbers 20:12 NIV). So instead of entering the Promised Land with his people, Moses died within eyesight of the land God had promised His people. Someone else got to finish what Moses had started.

Obedience to *all* God's commands should be of the utmost importance for the man of God. Remember: God blesses those who follow His instructions and finish well for Him.

Pray:

Father, may I always obey You fully.

Our Source of Forgiveness

Read Luke 7:36-50

Key Verses:

He said to her, "Your sins are forgiven." And those who sat for dinner with Him began to say to themselves, "Who is this who also forgives sins?"
LUKE 7:48–49 SKJV

Understand:

- What does Jesus' short parable of the moneylender tell us about God's willingness to forgive our sins?
- What does this passage show about the proper attitude toward those who have lived a sinful life?

Apply:

In an account recorded in Luke 7, Jesus showed dinner guests at the home of a Jewish religious leader named Simon that He had come to forgive and save not just those of high social standing—you know, the "good" people—but even the worst of sinners living the worst of lives.

As Jesus and the rest of the guests sat down to eat, a particularly notorious sinner—an unnamed woman who was very likely a prostitute—arrived at Simon's home, and straightaway she approached Jesus and began washing His feet with her tears, drying them with her hair, and kissing them and anointing them with ointment.

Clearly, this woman knew who she was, but more importantly, she showed that she knew who Jesus was and what He could do for her. Because she knew, she courageously entered the home of a powerful religious leader and showed her love for Jesus, the man who had the authority to forgive her many sins.

This sinful woman set an example for any man who knows he needs God's mercy and forgiveness. First, she went to great lengths to put herself before the one and only source of forgiveness and cleansing. Second, she expressed her deep gratitude for what only He could do for her.

Pray:

Lord Jesus, thank You for Your willingness to forgive even the worst of sinners, including me.

By Faith, Not Works

Read Romans 4:1-13

Key Verses:

If, in fact, Abraham was justified by works, he had something to boast about—but not before God. What does Scripture say? "Abraham believed God, and it was credited to him as righteousness."

Romans 4:2–3 NIV

Understand:

- Why could Abraham not glory in his justification before God?
- How can you increase your faith in the God who always keeps His promises?

Apply:

Part of our fallen human state is the common belief that we can earn our way into heaven by being a good person, by making sure that our good deeds outweigh the bad. But that is not what the Bible teaches, including this study's scripture reading, which features the justification of Abraham before God.

As the original patriarch of the Hebrew nation, Abraham holds a special place in the hearts of Jewish people and Christians alike. He is still revered as an example of righteous living. Not only that, he is an Old

Testament example of what many erroneously believe is just a New Testament concept: justification by faith.

Justification is an unmerited, free gift of God that is the result of faith, not our own goodness or works (Ephesians 2:8–9). This is also reflected in Genesis 15:6 (SKJV), which says that Abraham "believed in the LORD, and He counted it to him for righteousness."

In Romans 4:1–13, the apostle Paul applied the truths and blessings of the life of Abraham to New Testament Christians, showing us that our justification is based on faith alone, not anything good or meritorious about us.

So express your gratitude daily to the God who did for you what you could never do for yourself. Make it a goal to tell others of His amazing grace and generosity too.

Pray:

Thank You, Jesus, for doing for humanity, including me, what no man could do for himself.

Called to Intercede

Read 1 Samuel 12:18–25

Key Verse:

"As for me, far be it from me that I should sin against the Lord by failing to pray for you. And I will teach you the way that is good and right."

1 Samuel 12:23 NIV

Understand:

- For whom do you believe God wants you to begin praying today?
- How can you best begin a prayer life marked by consistent intercession?

Apply:

In 1 Samuel 12, the beloved prophet-judge Samuel gives his farewell address to the people of Israel, who had sinned against God by demanding that Samuel appoint a king to rule over them. The people had their king, and Samuel knew that God was not pleased about it. Nonetheless, Samuel pledged to pray for the people of Israel, even stating that to do otherwise would be a sin "against the Lord."

Samuel understood something we men need to lay hold of today, namely that men of God have the wonderful privilege—and the solemn responsibility—to come before the Lord and pray for others, to continually *intercede* for them.

John 17 gives an account of Jesus praying the perfect intercessory prayer for His disciples, who would be charged with taking His message of salvation throughout the world, and for all who would later know Him as their Lord and Savior.

Yet again, Jesus set a perfect example for us to follow.

What an awesome privilege it is to be welcome at the foot of the throne of our loving Creator to intercede on behalf of those He has placed in our lives!

Pray:

Jesus, You have called me to intercede on behalf of others—my family, my friends, my coworkers, my neighbors, and my brothers and sisters in You. May I never sin against You by neglecting such an important privilege and responsibility.

Self-Awareness

Read Genesis 32:1-12

Key Verses:

Jacob prayed, "O God of my grandfather Abraham, and God of my father, Isaac—O Lord, you told me, 'Return to your own land and to your relatives.' And you promised me, 'I will treat you kindly.' I am not worthy of all the unfailing love and faithfulness you have shown to me, your servant."

Genesis 32:9–10 NLT

Understand:

- Why do you think God loves you and saved you?
- What does your salvation tell you about God's nature?

Apply:

It might seem a little counterintuitive, but the closer we draw to Jesus Christ, the more aware we become of our own sinfulness and unworthiness before God. That's not to say that we engage in self-condemnation, only that we realize that we are sinners saved by grace and that only God's goodness and love can make us worthy in His eyes.

Consider the biblical patriarch Jacob.

Early in his life, Jacob was not a good man. He wanted what he wanted, and he showed himself willing to lie, cheat, and deceive to get it. Yet God loved this man and used him to help accomplish His very important purposes.

At one point in his life, Jacob seemed to come to the realization that he wasn't worthy of the goodness God had extended to him: "I am not worthy of all the unfailing love and faithfulness you have shown to me, your servant."

The truth of the matter is that none of us is worthy to receive anything good from the Lord. But God is gracious and loving, and He specializes in doing good for and through the unworthy.

Pray:

Gracious Lord, I know that, like Your servant Jacob, I'm not worthy of Your love, grace, and faithfulness. Help me to always remember that anything good You've given me is only because of Your goodness and love.

Integrity

Read Genesis 39:2–12

Key Verses:

"With me in charge," [Joseph] told her, "my master does not concern himself with anything in the house; everything he owns he has entrusted to my care. No one is greater in this house than I am. My master has withheld nothing from me except you, because you are his wife. How then could I do such a wicked thing and sin against God?"

GENESIS 39:8–9 NIV

Understand:

- What does the word *integrity* mean in the context of obedience to God's Word?
- How does your relationship with God help make you a man of integrity?

Apply:

Any employer does well to bring into his employ only people he can trust to do what is right, even when doing wrong would be a tempting, or even profitable, option. That is exactly why an Egyptian official named Potiphar put the young Hebrew Joseph in charge of his entire household.

God calls each of us to live lives of integrity and

to be careful to make choices worthy of a man who is part of His heavenly family. Joseph understood the importance of making choices that pleased the Lord, even when he might have gotten away with making a wrong one.

Potiphar's wife had access to Joseph, and she tried desperately to seduce him. But Joseph resisted Mrs. Potiphar—to the point of running away from her when she grabbed his cloak and tried to restrain him. Though Joseph had done nothing wrong, he was still thrown in jail. But because he acted with integrity, he remained on track to be used greatly in God's service and plans.

We should all be like Joseph, striving to always do what is right in God's eyes simply because it is right.

Pray:

Father in heaven, I want to be so committed to You and Your Word that I won't even think of sinning against You.

Overcoming the World

Read 1 John 5:1–12

Key Verse:

Who is it that overcomes the world except the one who believes that Jesus is the Son of God?

1 John 5:5 ESV

Understand:

- What does John mean by "the world"?
- In what ways does this world and its values bring you trouble and temptation?

Apply:

Shortly before He was arrested, Jesus issued this warning to His disciples: "In this world you will have trouble" (John 16:33 NIV). Jesus wanted His closest followers to know that being His disciples didn't mean that their lives here on earth would be easier. In fact, in some ways it would make life this side of heaven even more difficult.

But Jesus quickly followed His warning with this wonderful promise: "But take heart! I have overcome the world" (John 16:33 NIV). This promise reflects the ironclad truth that no matter how difficult life becomes, we can live as overcomers when we abide in Him.

Until Jesus returns and sets all things right, the devil has mostly free rein on this earth and in the lives of men who don't know the Lord. But the apostle John wrote that those of us who continue growing in our faith will overcome him and the world (1 John 2:13–14).

First John 5:5 tells us that there is but one way to overcome the world, and that is by placing our trust in Jesus, the Son of God. Through our faith in the Lord Jesus Christ—meaning believing in our hearts that He is the Son of God sent to earth to rescue us from our sins—we are empowered to live lives that please God as we resist the draw of the world's ways.

In Him, we are more than conquerors (Romans 8:37)!

Pray:

Lord Jesus, this world brings me all sorts of trouble and temptation. But You have overcome the world, and that means that through You I can overcome the world as well.

Forgiveness: Pay It Forward

Read Ephesians 4:25-32

Key Verses:

Get rid of all bitterness, rage, anger, harsh words, and slander, as well as all types of evil behavior. Instead, be kind to each other, tenderhearted, forgiving one another, just as God through Christ has forgiven you.

EPHESIANS 4:31–32 NLT

Understand:

- Do you presently feel angry over some past insult or slight?
- What can you do to let go of your anger or bitterness?

Apply:

In Matthew 18:23–35, Jesus spoke what is called the parable of the unmerciful servant. The nutshell version of this story goes like this: A heavily indebted servant has no means to repay what he owes, so he begs his master to be patient with him. But his master does him one better, canceling his whole debt and setting him free. The newly freed servant then goes to his fellow servant, demands repayment of a debt, and has him thrown in prison until he can pay him. When the unmerciful servant's master hears about what he has done. . .well, the story doesn't end well for him.

The point of the story is simple: Forgive, just as you've been forgiven.

The church is filled with people who sometimes say things they shouldn't, who hurt and offend us. If we're not careful, the sins of bitterness, rage, and anger can creep into our hearts, damaging our relationships with one another and with God.

This is why the apostle Paul enjoined us to treat one another with kindness, to be tenderhearted toward one another, and to forgive one another, just as God has forgiven us.

Forgiveness is a huge deal to God, so huge that He sent His Son to die so we can be forgiven. And when it's our turn to forgive, He wants us to always pay it forward to our brothers and sisters in Christ.

Pray:

Jesus, help me to always show kindness, compassion, and forgiveness to everyone, especially my fellow believers.

An Unlikely Servant

Read Matthew 9:9–13

Key Verse:

As Jesus was walking along, he saw a man named Matthew sitting at his tax collector's booth. "Follow me and be my disciple," Jesus said to him. So Matthew got up and followed him.

MATTHEW 9:9 NLT

Understand:

- Why do you think Jesus chose Matthew, a hated and notorious sinner, to follow Him?
- What do you think qualifies a man to follow and serve Jesus? Do you feel qualified?

Apply:

Most of us, if we were starting an important business or movement, wouldn't start by choosing society's also-rans or castoffs or those with sketchy pasts or reputations. But the Bible is filled with examples of God calling and using deeply flawed people to accomplish great things for Him.

Consider Matthew, the man who wrote the Gospel that bears his name. If any of us were starting a new social/religious movement, we wouldn't give this guy a second look. Matthew was a tax collector, which meant that he was at or near the top of the list when it came to the disdain of fellow Jews of that time. Being a tax collector, he—along with his friends—was a notorious sinner who cheated his own people and collaborated with the hated Roman government.

Anybody but *this* guy, right?

There's little doubt that the Jewish citizens in Matthew's hometown of Capernaum hated him. Jesus knew about Matthew's life, yet He stepped up to his tax-collecting booth and offered this irresistible invitation: "Follow me and be my disciple."

Matthew is an example of how a person's past, no matter how ugly it may be, does not disqualify him from following and serving Jesus. What Jesus calls us *to* matters far more than what He calls us *from*.

Pray:

Lord Jesus, thank You that following You has nothing to do with where I was in the past and everything to do with where You want to take me, now and in the future.

Loving Your Enemies

Read Matthew 5:38-48

Key Verses:

"You have heard that it has been said, 'You shall love your neighbor and hate your enemy.' But I say to you, love your enemies, bless those who curse you, do good to those who hate you, and pray for those who despitefully use you and persecute you."

MATTHEW 5:43–44 SKJV

Understand:

- What do you think it means to love your enemies? What does that kind of love look like?
- In what specific ways can you show love to people who don't love you back?

Apply:

In His Sermon on the Mount, Jesus delivered some radical teaching concerning how we who follow Him should deal with those who dislike us or mistreat us. This teaching was at once difficult and practical, and it was profoundly different from anything the people living in the land of Israel had ever heard.

Jesus' teaching in Matthew 5:38–48 goes against all human nature and logic. "Love your enemies"?

"Bless those who curse you"? "Do good to those who hate you"? "Pray for those who despitefully use you and persecute you"?

You can imagine people in the crowd that day thinking, *He can't be serious! Who would treat their enemies with such kindness?*

But Jesus *was* 100 percent serious, and He taught that those who proactively love their enemies mark themselves as true children of the living God.

Some people are not easy to love. They can be rude, demanding, surly, selfish, and unkind—and that's on their good days. Still others, through no fault of your own, just don't like you and treat you and speak of you negatively.

But Jesus has a message for us when we have to deal with difficult, unlovable people: Go out of your way and love them anyway.

Pray:

Lord Jesus, some people are hard to love. But I want to obey You and proactively love them anyway.

Built on the Rock

Read Matthew 7:21-29

Key Verses:

"Everyone then who hears these words of mine and does them will be like a wise man who built his house on the rock. And the rain fell, and the floods came, and the winds blew and beat on that house, but it did not fall, because it had been founded on the rock."

MATTHEW 7:24–25 ESV

Understand:

- Why is it so important that you build your life of faith on the solid foundation of Jesus and His teaching?
- What are the benefits of building your life on the solid rock?

Apply:

You don't have to be a master builder to know that a structure—a house, an office building, a hospital, or a production facility—built on a strong foundation has a much better chance of remaining upright in some natural disaster.

The same is true of our lives in Christ.

As Jesus closed His Sermon on the Mount, the greatest sermon ever preached, He encouraged and challenged His followers to build their lives on the teaching they had just heard—and by extension on Him.

Sometime after Jesus had died, risen from the dead, and returned to His Father in heaven, the apostle James wrote, "Do not merely listen to the word, and so deceive yourselves. Do what it says" (James 1:22 NIV).

If we build our lives on a weak foundation, then we're in for a life of frustration and defeat. But if our foundation is strong, we're sure to stand strong against the temptations, tests, and difficulties that life is sure to throw our way. That strong foundation is the Word of God, including the words of Jesus Himself. And we will be blessed when we do what it says.

Pray:

Jesus, thank You for being my rock and my foundation for a life built out of faith in You.

God's Heart for the Sinful

Read Ezekiel 18:21-32

Key Verses:

"Therefore, you Israelites, I will judge each of you according to your own ways, declares the Sovereign Lord*. Repent! Turn away from all your offenses; then sin will not be your downfall. Rid yourselves of all the offenses you have committed, and get a new heart and a new spirit. Why will you die, people of Israel? For I take no pleasure in the death of anyone, declares the Sovereign* Lord*. Repent and live!"*

Ezekiel 18:30–32 niv

Understand:

- Who in your life needs to hear God's message "Repent and live"?
- What do you think God wants you to do for lost, sinful people in your circle of influence?

Apply:

If you've read the book of Ezekiel from beginning to end, you've likely noticed that it is largely filled with pronouncements of God's judgment and wrath against various nations and people groups. But amid all the doom and gloom, God reveals His true heart of love toward even the most wicked. The key verses in this study recount God pleading with His people to turn away from their sins and warning them that they faced certain destruction for their wrongdoing. Then, at the end of this reading, He expressed His great love for humanity when He said, "I take no pleasure in the death of anyone, declares the Sovereign LORD. Repent and live!"

Hundreds of years later, the apostle Peter may have had the message of Ezekiel 18 in mind when he wrote, "The Lord is not slow in keeping his promise, as some understand slowness. Instead he is patient with you, not wanting anyone to perish, but everyone to come to repentance" (2 Peter 3:9 NIV).

Today, our heart toward the lost should be the same as God's, leading us to declare, "Repent and live!"

Pray:

Lord Jesus, I'm surrounded by people who need to turn to You so that they can live forever. Give me a heart like Yours toward the lost.

Blessings in Being "Poor"

Read Matthew 5:1-12

Key Verse:

"Blessed are the poor in spirit,
for theirs is the kingdom of heaven."
MATTHEW 5:3 NIV

Understand:

- What does it mean to you to be "poor in spirit"? Do you consider yourself poor in spirit?
- In what ways do you consider yourself strong and able? In what ways are you weak and needy?

Apply:

One of the themes throughout the pages of scripture is the benefits of humbly acknowledging our weaknesses, neediness, and helplessness when it comes to living a righteous life or doing anything for God apart from His loving-kindness and benevolence.

The scripture passage in this study features what have come to be known as the Beatitudes—meaning the series of statements of blessing Jesus spoke in the Sermon on the Mount in Matthew's Gospel. He began this amazing sermon by stating that the "poor in spirit" are blessed because the kingdom of heaven belongs to them.

The phrase "poor in spirit" means spiritual poverty. The poor in spirit are those who understand that they have nothing of value to offer to God and that they are spiritually poor before Him. They are those who confidently but humbly approach a holy but loving God as beggars with empty hands outstretched in hopes of receiving from Him.

We men don't like the thought of admitting that we are poor and needy. We tend to want to express strength and self-sufficiency, even when we attempt to do anything on behalf of God's eternal kingdom. But Jesus promises that when we humble ourselves and admit how little we have to offer God on our own, we will receive God's best blessings, including eternal life in the kingdom of heaven.

Pray:

Dear Jesus, thank You for giving me the best You have—simply because I humbly come to You with empty, outstretched hands. I am poor in spirit and have nothing to offer You but what You generously give me.

An Act of Faith. . . and Compassion

Read Luke 5:17-26

Key Verses:

Some men came carrying a paralyzed man on a mat and tried to take him into the house to lay him before Jesus. When they could not find a way to do this because of the crowd, they went up on the roof and lowered him on his mat through the tiles into the middle of the crowd, right in front of Jesus.

Luke 5:18–19 NIV

Understand:

- What heart attitude did the four men in Luke 5:17–26 demonstrate as they brought their paralyzed friend to Jesus?
- To what lengths would you be willing to go in order to bring a spiritually needy person to Jesus?

Apply:

Today's scripture passage doesn't identify by name the men who performed an incredible act of love and faith. But what's most important here isn't these men's names or identities but the lengths to which they went to get their friend in the presence of Jesus, the one they knew could help him.

As Jesus was teaching a big crowd in a house in Capernaum, these four men engaged in an incredible act of faith. . .and of heartwarming concern for their paralyzed friend. Rather than wait for a more convenient time to bring this poor soul to Jesus, the four tore a hole in the house's roof and lowered their friend to the one he desperately needed to see.

Do you have a friend who would go to such amazing lengths to bring a needy person to Jesus? Maybe more importantly, are you willing to *be* that kind of friend?

You don't have the power or authority to heal people and forgive their sins, but you know who does. So, what will you do to bring others to Him?

Pray:

Lord Jesus, give me a passion to bring others to You, the only one who can heal people, forgive them, and save them from their sins.

A Friend of Sinners

Read Mark 2:13-17

Key Verse:

When Jesus heard this, He told them, "Those who are well don't need a doctor, but the sick do need one. I didn't come to call the righteous, but sinners."

Mark 2:17 HCSB

Understand:

- How can you best follow the example Jesus set in Mark 2:13–17?
- How can you be a friend to sinners while avoiding joining them in sinful behavior?

Apply:

From the moment Jesus arrived here on earth, He remained laser focused on His reason for coming to live among us. This was a rescue mission focused on sinners, who desperately needed forgiveness and reconciliation with a holy but loving God, the God who highly valued creation but could not tolerate our sin.

After calling a tax collector named Levi (later known as Matthew) to follow Him, Jesus went to this sinner's home for dinner with him. . .and many other notorious sinners.

The Jewish people living in the land of Israel

despised tax collectors, as they were seen as collaborators with the Roman government. When the Jewish religious leaders witnessed Jesus dining with these lost souls, they were indignant. *Why does this man associate with such scum?* they wondered. But, as today's key verse suggests, Jesus knew He was right where He was needed in order to be what He had come to earth to be: a friend of sinners.

Jesus never consorted with sinners or joined with them in their wrongdoing. But He associated with them and befriended them, showing them the love and compassion they so desperately needed.

Do you consider yourself a friend of sinners—the kind of friend Jesus was to those who most needed Him?

Pray:

Jesus, help me to be a friend of sinners—
the kind of friend who loves them and
gently leads them into Your truth.

A Servant of Righteousness

Read Romans 6:11-18

Key Verses:

But thanks be to God that, though you used to be slaves to sin, you have come to obey from your heart the pattern of teaching that has now claimed your allegiance. You have been set free from sin and have become slaves to righteousness.

ROMANS 6:17–18 NIV

Understand:

- What are we believers dead to, according to Romans 6:11? To what/whom are we alive?
- What does it mean to you to be a slave to righteousness?

Apply:

In Romans 6, Paul addressed the way we believers are to live now that we've been adopted through Jesus into God's eternal family. No longer are we to live as slaves to sin, because we've been freed from its overwhelming power. That's why we can count ourselves "dead to sin but alive to God in Christ Jesus" (Romans 6:11 NIV).

This amazing truth presents each of us an important choice: Will we live our lives as servants of sin or servants of righteousness? Our choice comes down to whom we serve as our master. Will it be our sinful selves, or will it be Jesus, the one who died and was raised from the dead so that we could be delivered from the power of sin and eternal death? If Jesus is our Master, we will live in righteousness; but if we choose to be our own master, our lives will be governed by sin.

The Lord is our perfect Master but also our loving heavenly Father, our protector, and our source of comfort and strength and blessing. For that reason, we can live lives befitting heirs of His eternal kingdom.

That is the new life, the abundant life Jesus promised those who faithfully follow Him.

Pray:

Thank You, Jesus, for delivering me from the sin that controlled me before I knew You and for making me a true servant of righteousness.

Life as God's Adopted Child

Read Romans 8:14-21

Key Verses:

For as many as are led by the Spirit of God, they are the sons of God. For you have not received the spirit of bondage again to fear, but you have received the Spirit of adoption, by whom we cry, "Abba, Father!"

ROMANS 8:14–15 SKJV

Understand:

- Who are the rightful children of God, according to Romans 8:14?
- How can we address God as His adopted children?

Apply:

Jesus taught His followers the most important aspects of prayer when He spoke what we now call the Lord's Prayer (Matthew 6:9–13). He began His model for prayer by instructing us to address God as "our Father in heaven" (verse 9 NIV).

In Jesus' day, Jewish people didn't typically address God or refer to Him using the word *Father*. But Jesus did (many times over), and He taught His followers, including us today, to do the same. That's because He wanted us to understand that God is not just our Creator and Redeemer, not just the holy and all-powerful Lord of all, but our loving heavenly Father who desires a deeply personal, deeply loving relationship with us.

In Romans 8:14–21, Paul described life as an adopted child of God through Jesus. It's an intimate, joyful relationship with God the Father, one where the Christian has the privilege of addressing an almighty, holy God in the most familiar term, "Abba, Father!"

When you pray, remember that in Christ you are God's beloved child and He is your loving Father in heaven who wants an intimate relationship with the ones He calls His very own children.

Pray:

Thank You, Jesus, for making a way for me to be adopted into God's family and for giving me the privilege of addressing the all-holy, all-powerful God as "Father."

Jesus Our Intercessor

Read Hebrews 7:17–28

Key Verse:

Consequently, he is able to save to the uttermost those who draw near to God through him, since he always lives to make intercession for them.

Hebrews 7:25 ESV

Understand:

- When has a Christian brother promised to pray for you? How did you respond?
- In what ways does knowing that Jesus intercedes for you comfort and encourage you?

Apply:

Many of us have taken a degree of comfort during a particularly trying time when someone we know to be a dedicated prayer warrior made this simple pledge after hearing us out: *I'll be praying for you.*

The Bible encourages believers to pray fervently for others in an act called intercessory prayer. Not only that, the Word gives us a perfect example of interceding with God on behalf of others. In His High Priestly Prayer, Jesus interceded for all those who would believe in Him after He returned to heaven (John 17:20–24).

And in Hebrews 7:25, the writer promised his readers that this very day Jesus "lives to make intercession" for those who have come to God through Him.

What an amazing promise! The same Jesus who bridged the eternally wide gulf between us sinful humans and a holy God when He sacrificed Himself on a wooden cross still stands in the gap for us today, offering prayers for us—prayers pleading for our forgiveness and for God's blessings on us.

Everything Jesus said and did while He was on earth was to glorify God and benefit us. Today, as we endeavor to make an impact for God's eternal kingdom, Jesus sits at the right hand of God, asking that He comfort and strengthen us to face everything this life throws our way.

Pray:

Jesus, thank You for seeing my struggles and temptations and for taking them to the heavenly Father in prayer.

Who Am I?

Read Exodus 3:1-12

Key Verses:

But Moses said to God, "Who am I that I should go to Pharaoh and bring the Israelites out of Egypt?" And God said, "I will be with you. And this will be the sign to you that it is I who have sent you: When you have brought the people out of Egypt, you will worship God on this mountain."

Exodus 3:11–12 NIV

Understand:

- When was the last time you felt unqualified for something you knew you needed to do?
- How does knowing that God has promised to be with you affect your confidence?

Apply:

Moses had a heart for his Hebrew brothers and sisters languishing in Egypt while he hid out in Midian. After all, years before, he was forced to flee Egypt after he killed an Egyptian slave master for abusing a Hebrew slave.

Yes, Moses had a love for his people. What he didn't have, however, was confidence that he could do anything to help them. When God spoke from a burning bush and commanded Moses to return to Egypt and lead His people out of captivity, Moses answered with a long list of excuses, the first being "Who am I?"

Moses' encounter with God at the burning bush teaches us an important truth about how we should respond when God calls us to a difficult—even humanly impossible—task, and it's this: It's not about our human skills or abilities, or even about how we perceive ourselves. Rather, it's about knowing that our God has called us and promises to be with us and to give us everything we need to accomplish the task.

The Lord is your God, so it's not about you but about whom you serve.

Pray:

Lord, strengthen me and encourage me every day to do all You call me to do—especially when Your calling seems humanly impossible.

Through Jesus' Strength

Read Philippians 4:10-20

Key Verse:

For I can do everything through Christ, who gives me strength.
PHILIPPIANS 4:13 NLT

Understand:

- What taught Paul to conclude that he could do everything through Christ's strength?
- What specific difficult thing do you feel you need to depend on God's strength to do presently?

Apply:

In Philippians 4, Paul shared an important secret with his readers, a secret we present-day followers of Christ would do well to remember, namely that our present circumstances don't need to change how we approach life or how we depend on God.

Paul knew what it was like to endure difficulties of all sorts, but these things only led him to a deeper resolve to depend on Jesus for *all* things.

Nowhere in the Bible are we promised that serving Jesus is easy. During challenging times, we wouldn't be wrong if we were to look at what the Lord has for us to do and our own tough circumstances and then think, *I can't do it on my own!* Yet in Philippians 4:13, Paul wrote that he could do *everything* through the strength Jesus had given him.

That's a great promise for each of us, for it means that when we fully depend on Jesus in all things and in all circumstances, there's nothing we can't do for Him.

When you know that God is directing you to do something that seems too difficult to do in your own strength—like loving an unlovable someone or telling a skeptical friend about Jesus—don't tell yourself, "I can't!" Instead say, "I can do it through Christ, who gives me strength to do anything He has for me!"

Pray:

Jesus, thank You for being with me and helping me to think, talk, and live in ways that please You. I know I can't do it on my own, but with You I can do everything.

Our Perfect Example

Read Ephesians 5:1-13

Key Verse:

Live a life filled with love, following the example of Christ. He loved us and offered himself as a sacrifice for us, a pleasing aroma to God.

Ephesians 5:2 NLT

Understand:

- Why did Paul encourage believers to follow Christ's example? What does doing that look like in real life?
- What kinds of things did Jesus do to demonstrate His love to His followers?

Apply:

One of the many great things about the Bible is that it doesn't just tell us how to live; it shows us examples of how to do it. Let's start with the four Gospel accounts of the life of Jesus Christ. These four books include not just His commands and instructions for life but also the examples He set.

Jesus showed us how to live and how to love, from the moment He began His earthly ministry to the day He sacrificed Himself on a cross so that we could be saved from the power and consequences of our sin.

That's why He told His closest followers, "I have set you an example that you should do as I have done for you" (John 13:15 NIV). Today's key verse contains essentially the same message, encouraging us to "live a life filled with love."

As those who follow Jesus, we are commanded to be imitators of our heavenly Father, who sent us the perfect example of love in the person of His one and only Son. We reflect God by looking to Jesus, the one who is "the image of the invisible God" (Colossians 1:15 NIV).

Pray:

Lord Jesus, You were the perfect example of righteous living and committed loving during Your life here on earth. You loved me and sacrificed Yourself for me, and You want me to love others the same way. May I always follow Your example of how to live and love.

Mustard Seed Faith

Read Matthew 17:14-20

Key Verse:

"You don't have enough faith," Jesus told them. "I tell you the truth, if you had faith even as small as a mustard seed, you could say to this mountain, 'Move from here to there,' and it would move. Nothing would be impossible."

MATTHEW 17:20 NLT

Understand:

- How strong do you think your faith in God and His power is right now? How can you best strengthen your faith?
- What are the results of faith as small as a mustard seed?

Apply:

Jesus and His three closest disciples—Peter, James, and John—had returned to the rest of the disciples and a crowd after a short journey to the mountaintop, where Jesus was transfigured (Matthew 17:1–13). When they arrived, they found that the other nine had tried but failed to heal a demon-possessed boy.

Jesus voiced His frustration at what had just happened—or, more specifically, what *hadn't* happened—and then healed the boy with a simple verbal rebuke.

Now it was time to address the problem at hand.

After the disciples asked Jesus why they couldn't cast out the demon, He scolded them for their lack of faith and then told them that all it took was a very small amount of faith—"as small as a mustard seed"—to move mountains for the kingdom of God.

That's a great promise, right? And it shows us that what matters isn't the size of our faith but where that faith is placed.

When you place your faith—even if it seems very small—in your mighty God, there will be nothing you can't do for His eternal kingdom.

Pray:

Jesus, help me to remember that the size of my faith isn't nearly as important as where I put that faith. May my faith be 100 percent in You. I want to do great things for You!

The God of Comfort

Read 2 Corinthians 1:3–11

Key Verses:

Praise be to the God and Father of our Lord Jesus Christ, the Father of compassion and the God of all comfort, who comforts us in all our troubles, so that we can comfort those in any trouble with the comfort we ourselves receive from God.

2 Corinthians 1:3–4 NIV

Understand:

- How do you usually respond when you're enduring difficulties or suffering?
- When have you felt God's hand of comfort on you during a trying time?

Apply:

The apostle Paul knew something about needing comfort and encouragement. He had endured sometimes severe persecution for preaching the gospel message—beatings, stonings, imprisonments, and more. But he also knew that in all those troubles, he could turn to God—the same God who had sent His Son, Jesus, to earth to save him—and receive comfort, strength, and encouragement.

We modern-day Christian men are sure to go

through times of trouble. We may not endure the same kind of suffering the believers in the early church endured, but life here on twenty-first-century earth is far from perfect, so we're sure to go through difficulties.

The good news for those who follow Christ is that we can receive comfort from our heavenly Father—sometimes through the ministry of others, sometimes through the Holy Spirit's comforting work, and (most often) through Jesus, the ultimate source of comfort (2 Corinthians 1:5). What's more, God gives us the opportunity and the ability to pay it forward and lead others to Him, the God of all comfort.

Pray:

Jesus, You comfort me during difficult times—
sometimes through a trusted Christian friend
but always through time spent with You through
Your written Word. Thank You! Please use me as a
source of comfort and encouragement to others.

He Completes You

Read Philippians 1:3-11

Key Verses:

In all my prayers for all of you, I always pray with joy because of your partnership in the gospel from the first day until now, being confident of this, that he who began a good work in you will carry it on to completion until the day of Christ Jesus.

PHILIPPIANS 1:4–6 NIV

Understand:

- In what ways have you seen God change you to build you up in your faith?
- In what ways do you believe you need more growth in your relationship with Jesus?

Apply:

Can you think of a regret you have over not finishing something you started? Maybe it was some sort of restoration project that you started with great enthusiasm but abandoned when it became too difficult or too expensive. Or maybe you just lost interest at some point and gave up.

Many of us men live with the regret of failing to finish something we started. We may have started out with the best of intentions, but when the going got tough, we lost our enthusiasm and gave up.

In today's key verses, Paul wrote with great confidence that God always finishes what He starts when He saves someone through Jesus—even when the process takes much time and effort. That means that God will never give up on you, even when you feel like giving up on yourself.

We men often feel like giving up on something because it's too hard. But nothing is too hard for God. He is more than able to form you into the man He wants you to be, and He will do anything and everything it takes, for as long as it takes.

Pray:

Dear Jesus, sometimes I feel like I'm not changing fast enough, and I feel tempted to give up on myself. Remind me daily that You have promised to finish what You have started in me.

Search Me!

Read Psalm 139:17-24

Key Verses:

Search me, God, and know my heart; test me and know my anxious thoughts. See if there is any offensive way in me, and lead me in the way everlasting.

Psalm 139:23–24 NIV

Understand:

- How does knowing that God knows your heart make you feel?
- How do you think God would reveal "any offensive way" in you?

Apply:

Psalm 139 is a fantastic illustration of a man's deeply personal, deeply intimate relationship with his loving heavenly Father. It is a celebration of divine love and an invitation for the man's God to draw him ever closer each day.

In the first eighteen verses of this psalm, David praised his God both for knowing him so intimately and for thinking about him so constantly. David was absolutely basking in God's love as he wrote this psalm.

Still. . .David wanted more.

In today's key verses, David invited the Lord to

know him even better as he asked Him to "search me," "know my heart," "test me and know my anxious thoughts," and "see if there is any offensive way in me."

This was David asking the all-knowing, all-loving God to examine his very heart and show him any worries, lack of faith, or unrevealed sins. This was a man essentially saying, "Lord, I know You love me, so I'm asking You to help me be the man You've created me to be."

Today, God invites you to do the very same thing.

Pray:

Heavenly Father, help me to be so secure in Your love for me that I have the courage to boldly ask You to search me and let me know where I may be falling short. I thank You for knowing me so well and loving me so deeply.

When You Give

Read 2 Corinthians 9:6-15

Key Verses:

Remember this—a farmer who plants only a few seeds will get a small crop. But the one who plants generously will get a generous crop. You must each decide in your heart how much to give. And don't give reluctantly or in response to pressure. "For God loves a person who gives cheerfully."

2 CORINTHIANS 9:6–7 NLT

Understand:

- Do you consider yourself a cheerful giver or a reluctant giver?
- How can you become a more generous giver?

Apply:

In Jesus' day, the rich and powerful often went out of their way to make sure others knew about their giving so that they could be seen as generous. But Jesus called His followers to something different, teaching them, "When you give to the needy, sound no trumpet before you, as the hypocrites do in the synagogues and in the streets. . . . But when you give to the needy, do not let your left hand know what your right hand is doing, so that your giving may be in secret. And your Father who sees in secret will reward you" (Matthew 6:2–4 ESV).

Later, in his letter to the Corinthians, Paul encouraged followers of Christ to give liberally and as they are able but to do so out of a generous heart, promising his readers that God loves and blesses those who give willingly and cheerfully.

So bless others by giving as generously as you are able. But do so privately and without seeking human recognition. When you do just that, God will bless you as you have blessed others.

Pray:

Jesus, I know You want me to be a cheerful giver. Help me to be a generous person who doesn't need human recognition when I give but knows that God sees when I give with the right motives.

One Way Only

Read Acts 4:1-12

Key Verse:

"Salvation is found in no one else, for there is no other name under heaven given to mankind by which we must be saved."

ACTS 4:12 NIV

Understand:

- What kind of defenses do men put up when you tell them about salvation through Jesus?
- How can you best present the truth of salvation through Jesus alone?

Apply:

If you want to offend some men, if you want to be labeled "narrow-minded" or "bigoted," then plainly state this biblical truth: Jesus is the only path to eternal salvation. Holding unflinchingly to the biblical message that Jesus is the one and *only* way to peace with God and eternal salvation can lead to moments of discomfort. Speaking this exclusive message may cause you to lose relationships with people you care about.

We truly live in a "to each his own" world, don't we?

The apostle Peter, filled with the Holy Spirit,

courageously stated the truth about the way to eternal life, telling a council of Jewish religious leaders, who had the power to make things very difficult for him, that Jesus was the *one and only* path to eternal salvation.

In today's key verse, Peter echoed the message of the Lord Jesus Christ when He declared, "I am the way and the truth and the life. No one comes to the Father except through me" (John 14:6 NIV).

Modern thinking goes that a man can take any road to God as long as he follows it with sincerity and conviction. But the Bible teaches something entirely different, namely that Jesus is the only way. Don't forget to speak that message.

Pray:

Jesus, the message of salvation through You alone can be offensive to many. If I must offend anyone, let it be because I speak Your truth. May I always boldly speak the truth that You are the one and only way to salvation.

Christ's Representatives

Read Colossians 3:5–17

Key Verse:

And whatever you do or say, do it as a representative of the Lord Jesus, giving thanks through him to God the Father.
COLOSSIANS 3:17 NLT

Understand:

- What kinds of actions and attitudes does this study's scripture reading say you must avoid?
- What kinds of actions and attitudes does this study's scripture reading encourage you to engage in?

Apply:

In this study's scripture reading, the apostle Paul went to great lengths to let his readers know that those who make a profession of faith are to live and speak in ways far different from those who don't know Him. That means we are to avoid things such as sexual immorality, impurity, lust, greed, anger, rage, malice, slander, filthy language, and lying.

We should avoid these things—first, because they are displeasing to the Lord, and second, because they reflect badly on our Lord and what He has done for us.

Today's key verse tells us that God wants us to act as representatives of the Lord Jesus Christ in *everything we say* and *everything we do*. That means making sure that our every action and every word reflect our identities as followers of Jesus and children of the living God. It means not just avoiding the sins listed in Colossians 3:5–9 but also purposefully living according to the admonitions in verses 12–16.

Our first thoughts each morning should be of how we can best represent Jesus in everything we do and say, knowing that it's what God wants for us and what those around us need to see.

Pray:

Dear Jesus, I want to be a good representative for You in everything I do and in everything I say. Help me to reflect who I am in You every day.

Don't Be Complacent!

Read Hebrews 6:1–12

Key Verses:

We want each of you to show this same diligence to the very end, so that what you hope for may be fully realized. We do not want you to become lazy, but to imitate those who through faith and patience inherit what has been promised.

HEBREWS 6:11–12 NIV

Understand:

- What is the writer of Hebrews warning readers against in this study's scripture reading?
- How can you best continue growing in your faith?

Apply:

If there's one thing that will scuttle the career of an otherwise competent, talented man in any professional endeavor, it's complacency. Many a promising career has been ruined—or at least stunted—when a man adopts a complacent or lazy attitude.

The Bible repeatedly warns God's people against complacency, which can also be described as *spiritual laziness*. This study's key verses address this very issue, but in an encouraging way: "We want each of you to show this same diligence to the very end, so that what you hope for may be fully realized."

When you were first saved, God set you on a path that He never promised would be easy. On the contrary, this path would require patience, perseverance, and, yes, hard work before you could fully enjoy the fullness of His promised blessings. Indeed, being a victorious Christian is far from easy!

So even if your Christian life seems to be going well, be careful not to let your guard down. The life of faith requires that you're always ready for battle, that you're diligent, and that you persevere through the trials and temptations that are sure to come your way.

Pray:

Lord Jesus, may I never become complacent or lazy in my walk of faith or in my relationship with You. Rather, may I daily choose to push forward with diligence and commitment to You.

Loving Discipline

Read Hebrews 12:4-13

Key Verses:

Endure hardship as discipline; God is treating you as his children. For what children are not disciplined by their father? If you are not disciplined—and everyone undergoes discipline—then you are not legitimate, not true sons and daughters at all.

HEBREWS 12:7–8 NIV

Understand:

- What does the word *discipline* mean to you?
- What is the difference between discipline and punishment?

Apply:

You can always tell when another person's child has received loving discipline. They are usually well behaved, polite in how they talk and act toward others, and humble yet confident. A lack of discipline is equally easy to discern. An undisciplined child lacks self-control and often treats and speaks to others disrespectfully.

Which of those two children would you prefer to be around?

As a heavenly Father who loves us far more deeply

and more thoroughly than even the very best earthly dad, God makes sure never to withhold from us His loving hand of discipline. And while having His hand of discipline on us is never pleasant, it is evidence that we are His through Jesus Christ and that He loves us as His very own children.

When you are going through different kinds of difficulties, you can take comfort in knowing that the Lord can and does use those things to correct you, teach you, nurture you, and grow you into the man He intends you to be. In that sense, you can endure all sorts of difficulties, knowing that none of them will be wasted.

When you go through a time of discipline and correction, it is one of God's demonstrations of His Fatherly love. It means you are truly His and part of His eternal family. And it means He's preparing you to make a difference in the world around you.

Pray:

Thank You, Lord, for lovingly disciplining me so that I may become the man You want me to become.

Your Eternal Citizenship

Read Philippians 3:15-21

Key Verses:

Our citizenship is in heaven. And we eagerly await a Savior from there, the Lord Jesus Christ, who, by the power that enables him to bring everything under his control, will transform our lowly bodies so that they will be like his glorious body.

PHILIPPIANS 3:20–21 NIV

Understand:

- How does knowing that your true citizenship is in heaven help shape your life here on earth?
- What do you think heaven will be like? In what ways will you be changed as you take up residence there?

Apply:

When you received salvation through the Lord Jesus Christ, a lot of things changed for you. Your thinking changed, your priorities changed, your focus changed, and your approach to other people changed.

In addition to all those things—and perhaps more importantly—your *citizenship* changed. Yes, you are still a citizen of the nation, state, and city where you live. But as a man who follows Jesus Christ, your true citizenship is in heaven, where you will one day take up eternal residence with Jesus.

As American citizens, we have many rights and privileges conferred on us. But as Christian men, we now live in a home away from home here on earth. Knowing that, we can and should do all we can to influence individuals, our culture, and our government toward God and godly principles. But let us do those things thinking about our forever home in God's eternal kingdom.

We believers have so much to look forward to beyond this life on earth. Let us all live our lives here on earth with an eye that looks beyond the here and now.

Pray:

Lord Jesus, as an American man, I am a citizen of the United States. Much more importantly, though, I am a citizen of Your eternal kingdom in heaven.

Overcoming Temptation

Read 1 Corinthians 10:1-13

Key Verse:

No temptation has overtaken you except what is common to mankind. And God is faithful; he will not let you be tempted beyond what you can bear. But when you are tempted, he will also provide a way out so that you can endure it.

1 CORINTHIANS 10:13 NIV

Understand:

- Do you ever feel weak against temptation? How do you find strength?
- Why do you think God allows Christian men to be tempted?

Apply:

When you first started your life of faith in Jesus Christ, you might have believed you wouldn't need to worry about temptation. After all, Jesus promises to give you strength to overcome anything the devil and this world throws your way, right? But it probably wasn't long before you realized that knowing Jesus doesn't automatically remove all temptation to sin. In fact, the devil will work overtime to cause you to sin so he can derail you from God's plans for you—just like he once tried to do with Jesus (see Matthew 4:1–11).

We're all tempted to sin, and our spiritual enemy knows our tendencies and weaknesses. That's why Jesus included the words "lead us not into temptation" in His model prayer (Matthew 6:13 NIV). Jesus didn't mean that God could ever lead us into temptations to sin (James 1:13–14). His was a simple plea for God to protect us and strengthen us against the temptation to stray.

God has promised to keep us from temptation too strong for us to handle. When we access that promise in prayer, we do our part to avoid temptation before it can overtake us.

Pray:

Lord Jesus, temptation will always be a part of my life here on earth. Please give me wisdom to avoid temptation and the strength to overcome it so that I may glorify You every day.

Ultimate Victory

Read 1 Corinthians 15:50-58

Key Verses:

The sting of death is sin, and the power of sin is the law. But thanks be to God! He gives us the victory through our Lord Jesus Christ.

1 Corinthians 15:56–57 NIV

Understand:

- As a follower of Jesus Christ, how should you view physical death?
- What does the Bible mean when it says that "the sting of death is sin"?

Apply:

Living in a fallen world, we're all far too familiar with the horrible effects of sin. On different levels, we know death, we know sickness, we know addiction, we know bondage, and we know hopelessness.

The creation story in Genesis 1–2 tells us that God placed us humans in a perfect world where we would never experience sickness and death and where we could enjoy perfect fellowship with our loving Creator. But when Adam and Eve chose sin over obedience, they brought death and destruction and suffering into the human experience. Worse yet, their sin brought separation between a holy God and His most prized creation.

The consequences of Adam and Eve's sin were immediately evident, and they've continued unabated ever since then, for we are all born under the curse of sin and death.

But God had a plan to reconcile sinful humanity to Himself. Almost immediately after Adam and Eve sinned, God announced that He would send a Savior into the world to defeat sin and death once and for all (Genesis 3:14–15).

When Jesus died and was raised from the dead, He broke the power of sin and death for everyone who would believe in Him. We have victory in the Lord Jesus Christ and eternal life in a forever home with Him in heaven.

Pray:

Thank You, Jesus, for defeating the power of sin and death and for giving me eternal life in heaven.

Send Me!

Read Isaiah 6:1-8

Key Verse:

Then I heard the voice of the Lord saying, "Whom shall I send? And who will go for us?" And I said, "Here am I. Send me!"

Isaiah 6:8 niv

Understand:

- Whom do you have a passion to minister to?
- Do you sense God's call to minister to particular individuals or people groups?

Apply:

The prophet Isaiah had seen the glory of the Lord one day in the temple, and it terrified him. He saw flying angelic creatures and heard them singing praises to the Lord. The temple was filled with smoke, and its doorposts shook at the sound of their voices.

"Woe to me!" Isaiah exclaimed. "I am ruined! For I am a man of unclean lips, and I live among a people of unclean lips, and my eyes have seen the King, the Lord Almighty" (Isaiah 6:5 niv).

God's angels purified Isaiah's lips and made him fit to serve and to preach the Lord's truth to His people.

Now ready to speak God's message to His hard-hearted people, Isaiah eagerly volunteered when God asked, "Whom shall I send? And who will go for us?"

Does your heart ever ache over the hurting, needy people in your neighborhood, in our nation, or around the world? Do you ever find yourself grieving over the lostness of humanity, wondering what you can do to reach them with the message of salvation through Jesus Christ? If you answered yes to either of those questions, then it may be that God is preparing you and calling you to some kind of service—just as He did the prophet Isaiah.

God has something for you to do for His kingdom. He has given you gifts and can enable you to do what He's called you to do.

Pray:

Father, please give me a heart to minister to those who need to hear about You.

Speaking the Message

Read Mark 16:9-20

Key Verse:

He said to them, "Go into all the world and preach the gospel to all creation."
MARK 16:15 NIV

Understand:

- Why should you make it a goal to share the gospel message with others?
- How can you best prepare yourself to share your faith?

Apply:

Someone (it's not known for sure who) once famously said, "Preach the gospel at all times; if necessary, use words." While the message of this quote—that our lives should reflect Jesus in all ways—has great validity, the deeper truth is that Jesus has called us to use words to communicate the gospel message. As the apostle Peter wrote, "Always be prepared to give an answer to everyone who asks you to give the reason for the hope that you have" (1 Peter 3:15 NIV).

In today's key verse, Jesus spoke to His disciples about what is called the Great Commission. This was Jesus' marching orders to take His message of salvation to the world around them after He returned to heaven.

And that call to preach the gospel applies to His followers today. That means you have the privilege—and the responsibility—to tell people in your sphere of influence about how they can have peace with God and eternal life through Jesus Christ.

You don't have to be a missionary, pastor, or evangelist to be qualified to tell others about salvation through Jesus. Just ask God to guide you toward people who need to hear about Him and to prepare your heart to speak up when He gives you the opportunity to speak His name.

Pray:

Lord Jesus, I want to help others to know You as I know You. Help me to keep my eyes and ears open for opportunities to "preach the gospel" to people around me.

Divine Forgetfulness

Read Hebrews 8:3-12

Key Verse:

"For I will forgive their wickedness and will remember their sins no more."
HEBREWS 8:12 NIV

Understand:

- Do you ever struggle with guilt and condemnation over some past wrongdoing? Why do you think that is?
- Where do you think you can take your guilt and self-condemnation for relief?

Apply:

Many Christian men look back on their life before Christ and cringe when they think of certain lifestyles or incidents. They're pretty sure that God has forgiven them, but still, they wonder how He can forgive and forget that one thing they themselves can't seem to shake.

But in today's key verse, the writer repeated an astounding promise from Jeremiah 31:31–34, namely that the Lord not only *forgives* our sins—He *forgets* them.

We fallen human beings often have a difficult time forgiving, let alone forgetting, wrongs done to us. Without intervention and help from above, we tend to hang on to anger, which leads to bitterness, which leads. . .nowhere good. We can be grateful that it's not that way with our heavenly Father.

It might seem strange that an all-knowing, all-powerful God could forget anything, including our sin. But Hebrews 8:12 and Jeremiah 31:31–34 indicate a purposeful act of the will on His part to erase our past sins from His thoughts.

Hanging on to guilt and self-condemnation over past wrongdoing can stunt your spiritual growth and keep you from living a life that makes a difference for God's eternal kingdom. But your loving heavenly Father has promised He will no longer remember even the worst of your past sins. Knowing that, why should you?

Pray:

Lord Jesus, help me to rest in the wonderful truth that all my past sins are forgiven and forgotten. Thank You for Your amazing mercy!

A Fitting Response

Read Romans 12:1-8

Key Verses:

Therefore I beseech you, brothers, by the mercies of God, that you present your bodies as a living sacrifice, holy, acceptable to God, which is your reasonable service. And do not be conformed to this world, but be transformed by the renewing of your mind, that you may prove what is that good and acceptable and perfect will of God.

Romans 12:1–2 SKJV

Understand:

- What does it mean to you to offer your body as a living sacrifice? What would be the result of doing that?
- What did Paul mean by "be transformed by the renewing of your mind"? How does this transformation take place?

Apply:

In the Old Testament, God laid out a system of sacrifices that allowed His people to receive forgiveness for their sins. Those sacrifices would one day be replaced with a onetime, perfect sacrifice—when Jesus went to the cross to die for the sins of all humankind.

In this study's scripture reading, Paul encouraged the Christians in Rome to offer up to God not just their souls and lives and wills as living sacrifices but their very bodies. In other words, they were to give to God their entire being for Him to do with as He desired.

He desires that same sacrifice from us believers today.

The apostle also encouraged those in the Roman church to resist conformity to the world and to allow God to transform their minds so that their thinking would reflect the "good and acceptable and perfect will of God."

Finally, Paul encouraged humility for the Roman believers, for God loves humility and resists the proud. That humility would serve them as they each played their part in serving one another.

Pray:

Lord Jesus, I present my whole self to You as a living sacrifice. Do with me as You will!

An Empathetic High Priest

Read Hebrews 4:12-16

Key Verses:

For we do not have a high priest who is unable to empathize with our weaknesses, but we have one who has been tempted in every way, just as we are—yet he did not sin. Let us then approach God's throne of grace with confidence, so that we may receive mercy and find grace to help us in our time of need.

HEBREWS 4:15–16 NIV

Understand:

- What assurance does knowing that Jesus empathizes give you?
- How confident do you feel when you approach the Lord with your needs?

Apply:

Do you ever feel like you're struggling through life here on earth completely alone, like God has left you to fight against sin, against fear, against discouragement on your own? You need someone to talk to, someone who understands your faith struggles, your temptations, and your battles in the mind.

When you feel that way (and even the godliest

of men do at times), this study's key verses can give you blessed assurance that you have a Savior who truly gets you.

When you face times of trouble, when you feel weak, when your faith is waning, when you feel overwhelming temptation. . .the writer of Hebrews said to turn to the High Priest, Jesus: "Let us then approach God's throne of grace with confidence, so that we may receive mercy and find grace to help us in our time of need."

You're truly never alone! Not only that, you can also approach God's throne with confidence, knowing that He wants to help you.

Pray:

High Priest Jesus, whenever I feel like I'm struggling through life on my own, remind me that You are with me on the deepest level. Thank You for being a Savior I can talk to, a Savior who understands me and my struggles and weaknesses. I have You, so I never have to struggle alone.

Hidden Sin?

Read Numbers 32:20-30

Key Verse:

"But if you fail to do this, you will be sinning against the LORD; and you may be sure that your sin will find you out."
NUMBERS 32:23 NIV

Understand:

- How important is it to God that you faithfully keep your word and honor your agreements? How important is it to you?
- Why should you never try to hide your sin from the Lord?

Apply:

The Israelites were drawing closer to the Promised Land, and the tribes of Reuben and Gad saw an excellent opportunity for themselves in the area south of the Sea of Galilee, just outside the Promised Land. They believed it would be a great area to raise their families and to farm and keep their livestock. The two tribes wanted this land, so they approached Moses and made him an offer: If the men of Reuben and Gad pledged to lead the Israelites in taking the Promised Land, then they could settle in the land they desired.

It was an audacious offer, one that benefited all parties involved, and Moses accepted it. But he also warned them that if they failed to hold up their end of the agreement, they would be sinning against God, and God would know it. . .and they would suffer the consequences for their sin.

There are two things we need to remember about sin, the first being that we can never hide it from God. Moses himself wrote, "You have set our iniquities before you, our secret sins in the light of your presence" (Psalm 90:8 NIV). Secondly, sin—whether it's a failure to keep our word, sexual immorality, or any kind of idolatry—always has consequences.

God takes all sin very seriously—and so should we.

Pray:

Lord God, may I never try to hide my sin.
Please keep my heart soft and receptive to Your Word
so that I always remember the seriousness of sin.

A New Heart

Read Ezekiel 11:14–25

Key Verses:

"And I will give them singleness of heart and put a new spirit within them. I will take away their stony, stubborn heart and give them a tender, responsive heart, so they will obey my decrees and regulations. Then they will truly be my people, and I will be their God."

EZEKIEL 11:19–20 NLT

Understand:

- In what specific ways does God change a man when he turns to Jesus in faith?
- What do you think are the results of the new heart God has placed within you?

Apply:

What an amazing set of promises in this study's scripture reading! As punishment for their sins, God had sent His people away from the homeland He had given them and forced them to live in foreign lands. But the Lord was far from finished with His people. One day He would not only bring them out of exile; He would revive them by replacing their hard heart with "a tender, responsive heart" so that they could truly be His people and He could be their God.

That's a miracle of the highest order, and it's not unlike what the Lord does for a man when he turns to Jesus Christ for salvation. When a man is first saved, God gives him a new heart that is tender toward Him, that truly loves Him, that wants to please Him in every way.

The apostle Paul wrote that "anyone who belongs to Christ has become a new person. The old life is gone; a new life has begun!" (2 Corinthians 5:17 NLT). This means that we followers of Jesus are more than "new and improved" versions of our old selves; we are, in the most important ways, transformed so that we're no longer what we were before but something radically different.

Pray:

Thank You, Jesus, for transforming me, not just changing me, and for making me a new person.

Handling Opposition

Read 2 Timothy 3:10–17

Key Verses:

In fact, everyone who wants to live a godly life in Christ Jesus will be persecuted, while evildoers and impostors will go from bad to worse, deceiving and being deceived.

2 Timothy 3:12–13 NIV

Understand:

- When was the last time someone expressed disapproval or spoke negatively to you because you spoke out for Jesus?
- How can you make the Bible a bigger part of your life?

Apply:

How do you respond when you are faced with opposition for speaking out about Jesus? Do you feel discouraged or angry? Do you wonder if God is looking out for you or if He truly wants to use you to further His heavenly kingdom?

The apostle Paul was as supremely confident in God's calling as anyone we read about in scripture, and he accomplished mind-blowing things for the Lord. And yet he also endured persecution, the likes of which we today can hardly imagine.

In 2 Timothy 3:12–13, Paul made us Christian men a promise most of us probably wish we could overlook. Yes, we want to "live a godly life in Christ Jesus," but we'd just as soon skip the persecution part. But we can trust Paul when he said we'll be persecuted for living godly lives. After all, Paul knew about these things (see 2 Timothy 3:11).

In modern-day America, we Christians don't face the kind of persecution Paul suffered for Jesus' sake. But no matter what form of persecution we face, we can rest in this promise from the mouth of Jesus: "God blesses you when people mock you and persecute you and lie about you and say all sorts of evil things against you because you are my followers" (Matthew 5:11 NLT).

Pray:

Jesus, when I am criticized or mocked for following You, help me to remember that God blesses those who face all sorts of persecution.

Loving the Undeserving

Read Luke 6:27-36

Key Verses:

"But to you who are listening I say: Love your enemies, do good to those who hate you, bless those who curse you, pray for those who mistreat you."
Luke 6:27–28 NIV

Understand:

- How do you usually feel toward someone who has spoken ill of you or intentionally done something to hurt you?
- How can you best show your love to someone who mistreats you—in word or in deed?

Apply:

It's not always easy to treat people with kindness or to do good to them. Some people are just difficult to love, and sometimes it's all we can do just to show them simple tolerance, let alone truly love them.

But Jesus calls His followers to a radical kind of love, a love that does good for them and prays for them even when, humanly speaking, they deserve anything and everything but acts of love and kindness.

Think about some of the ways you can love others,

even the most unlovable, even those who have spoken unkind words to or about you, even those who have thoughtlessly or maliciously mistreated you. Do you go out of your way to speak kind words to them and to perform intentional acts of kindness for them?

If you find yourself struggling to love the unlovable and do good for them, just remember that Jesus did the kindest, most loving thing in all of history when He died for a sinner like you. When He did that, He set an example for you to follow every day.

Pray:

Lord Jesus, I confess that there have been times when I have been tempted to lash out at someone who has spoken unkind words or mistreated me. But You have called me to something better. Help me to love those who don't deserve my love.

The Law of Forgiveness

Read Matthew 18:21-35

Key Verses:

Then Peter came to Him and said, "Lord, how often shall my brother sin against me and I forgive him? Up to seven times?" Jesus said to him, "I do not say to you, up to seven times, but up to seventy times seven."

MATTHEW 18:21–22 SKJV

Understand:

- What makes it so difficult to forgive someone who has wronged you in some way?
- What did Jesus mean when He told Peter that he should forgive "up to seventy times seven"?

Apply:

Forgiveness is important to God, so important that He gave His Son, Jesus Christ, as a sacrifice for our sins so that we could be forgiven and then welcomed into His eternal kingdom.

The Bible is filled with accounts of God forgiving those who have sinned against Him. But it doesn't stop there. In today's key verses, Jesus taught Peter and the rest of the disciples a valuable lesson about forgiving others.

Peter probably thought he had impressed Jesus when he asked Him if he should forgive someone who had sinned against him up to seven times. But the disciples were astonished when Jesus took forgiveness to a whole new level, instructing them to forgive others "seventy times seven" times.

Jesus was calling His followers to a life marked by unlimited forgiveness for others, a life well defined by these words from the apostle Paul: "Be kind and compassionate to one another, forgiving each other, just as in Christ God forgave you" (Ephesians 4:32 NIV).

This is a radical brand of forgiveness that chooses to release others from the guilt of their offenses completely, repeatedly, and without reservation—the same way our Father in heaven has forgiven us.

Pray:

Jesus, You have forgiven me for more acts of sin and rebellion than I can count. May I always forgive others the way You have forgiven me—completely and without limitation.

Ask, Seek, Knock

Read Luke 11:1-13

Key Verses:

"And I say to you, ask, and it shall be given to you; seek, and you shall find; knock, and it shall be opened to you. For everyone who asks receives, and he who seeks finds, and to him who knocks it shall be opened."

LUKE 11:9–10 SKJV

Understand:

- Why do you think it's important to address God as "Father"?
- What do verses 9–10 in today's scripture reading tell you about God's desire to hear and answer your prayers?

Apply:

Have you ever stopped to consider what an awesome privilege it is to go to God in prayer, to "approach God's throne of grace with confidence" (Hebrews 4:16 NIV) and present our requests to Him?

In today's scripture reading, Jesus spoke some amazing instructions concerning effective prayer. His twelve disciples had just watched their Master as He prayed, and it stirred something inside them; they wanted to know how He prayed with such power, how He bound

His heart and mind to His Father. *How can we pray like Him?* they wondered. Then they opened their mouths and said, "Lord, teach us to pray" (Luke 11:1 SKJV).

Jesus was pleased by the disciples' request, and He spoke to them what we know today as the Lord's Prayer, not necessarily so that they could recite it word for word as they prayed but so that they could model their own prayers after what He had said about praying to their perfect Father in heaven.

Furthermore, He taught them the importance of persistent prayer—and God's willingness to honor and answer such prayers with His very best.

Pray:

Thank You, Jesus, for teaching Your followers how to pray. Thank You for giving me the privilege of coming to God in prayer. May I never take that privilege for granted, and may I never neglect to take advantage of it, even for one day.

"Take Courage!"

Read Mark 6:45-52

Key Verses:

When they saw him walking on the lake,
they thought he was a ghost. They cried out,
because they all saw him and were terrified.
Immediately he spoke to them and said,
"Take courage! It is I. Don't be afraid."
MARK 6:49–50 NIV

Understand:

- How do you think you should respond when you are beset by life's inevitable headwinds?
- How does knowing that Jesus is with you help you handle fear?

Apply:

Jesus' disciples had just come off the spiritual high of witnessing Jesus feed thousands of people with five loaves of bread and two fish (Mark 6:30–44). But they were in for a rough evening after this miracle.

After feeding all those people, Jesus sent the disciples away, commanding them to board their boat and cross the Sea of Galilee while He stayed behind to pray. But a powerful headwind began pushing relentlessly at their boat, making for slow going on their way toward the far shore.

The disciples must have wondered if things would be different for them had Jesus been there with them. Jesus could see His followers' struggles, and He arrived on the scene—walking on the water! The disciples were terrified when they saw Jesus, thinking He was a ghost. But Jesus calmed the disciples' fears with words of comfort and then boarded the boat. Immediately the wind died down.

When you find yourself struggling against the sometimes overwhelming headwinds of life, remember that Jesus sees and cares—and that He will never leave you alone to live in futility.

Pray:

Jesus, I know I'll sometimes face the frightening headwinds of life. But when You are with me, I know I don't have to give in to debilitating fear. Help me keep my eyes on You always.

Childlike Faith

Read Matthew 18:1-6

Key Verses:

"So anyone who becomes as humble as this little child is the greatest in the Kingdom of Heaven. And anyone who welcomes a little child like this on my behalf is welcoming me."

MATTHEW 18:4–5 NLT

Understand:

- What does it mean to be "the greatest in the Kingdom of Heaven"?
- What does it mean to you to become "as humble at this little child"? How can you become like a little child in your life of faith?

Apply:

One day, the disciples approached Jesus and asked Him who was greatest in God's kingdom. His answer probably surprised the Twelve, who likely expected Him to say something about some giant of the faith whose confidence allowed him to accomplish great things for the Lord. Instead, He called a small child to Him and told them, "Truly I tell you, unless you change and become like little children, you will never enter the kingdom of heaven" (Matthew 18:3 NIV).

This was one of Jesus' most profound object lessons concerning humility and faith, and it still applies to us today, for it teaches us the kind of faith God requires from each of us in order to enter His glorious eternal kingdom. It's a faith that prompts us to come to Him in humility, knowing that we are needy and have nothing to offer in return but simple, childlike trust. It leads us to approach Him with open, empty hands, knowing that He desires to do good for those who come to Him in meekness.

How would you describe your faith in God today? Is it a childlike faith? In what ways do you think it needs to change if you desire not just to enter but to become great in the kingdom of heaven?

Pray:

Father in heaven, help me to come to You daily with childlike faith—trusting, helpless, openhearted, and fully dependent on You for everything.

Be Ready!

Read 1 Peter 3:13-22

Key Verse:

In your hearts honor Christ the Lord as holy, always being prepared to make a defense to anyone who asks you for a reason for the hope that is in you; yet do it with gentleness and respect.

1 PETER 3:15 ESV

Understand:

- How has your faith in Jesus shaped your attitudes and actions?
- How can you best prepare yourself to share your faith with others?

Apply:

A life lived in Jesus Christ is a life that demonstrates love, joy, peace, patience, kindness, and other qualities Paul called the fruit of the Spirit (Galatians 5:22–23). These qualities should be evident in the believer's life regardless of his present circumstances. And when our attitudes and actions in the face of suffering and difficulties still exhibit these fruits, other men will notice, and that could very well lead to how-do-you-do-it questions.

Before He departed earth to return to His Father in heaven, Jesus assigned His disciples the task of taking the message of salvation to the world around them. Jesus had done amazing things in these men's lives, and He wanted them to share what they knew and what they had with many others.

Today, Jesus calls you to do the very same thing.

The Lord has done amazing things for you—starting with saving you and preparing a place for you in heaven. He also gave you His Holy Spirit, who helps you to live a Christlike life and who empowers you to share your faith with others.

Because you follow Jesus, people should see in your life evidence of what He has done for you. Knowing that should motivate you to always be ready to gently speak the promise of salvation through Him.

Pray:

Jesus, help me to be ready with an answer when others ask me questions about what You've done for me.

About the Author

Tracy M. Sumner is a freelance author, writer, and editor in Hillsboro, Oregon. An avid outdoorsman, he enjoys fly-fishing on world-class Oregon waters.